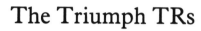

The Triumph TRs

The Triumph TRs

A collector's guide
by Graham Robson

GCPress Motor Racing Publications

MOTOR RACING PUBLICATIONS LTD
28 Devonshire Road, Chiswick, London W4 2HD, England

First published 1978
Reprinted 1978
Reprinted 1980
Second Edition 1981
Reprinted 1982
Reprinted 1983
Reprinted 1987

ISBN 0 900549 63 7

Photosetting by Zee Creative Ltd., London SW16
Printed in Great Britain by The Garden City Press Ltd.,
Letchworth, Hertfordshire

Contents

Introduction			6
Chapter 1	Ancestors and parentage	1800 and 2000, TRX and TR1	9
Chapter 2	The classic TR — 1953 to 1962	TR2, TR3, TR3A and TR3B	17
Chapter 3	The TR in transition — 1961 to 1967	TR4 and TR4A	33
Chapter 4	TRs in competition	Racing and rallying, including the Twin-Cams	49
Chapter 5	Six-cylinder TRs — 1967 to 1976	TR5, TR250 and TR6	70
Chapter 6	A new breed of TR	The TR7 range so far	85
Chapter 7	Prototypes and specials	Zoom, Italia, Francorchamps and others	100
Chapter 8	Buying an older TR	What to look for, restoration and the 'Best Buys'	112
Chapter 9	Spares and maintenance	Factory, TR Register and VTR facilities	116
Appendix A	Technical specification summaries — TR1 to TR8		121
Appendix B	Commission Number sequences — model by model		124
Appendix C	TR deliveries — 1953 to date		125
Appendix D	How fast? How economical? How heavy? Performance summary of TR models		127

Introduction

It is now 25 years since the Triumph TR sports car was born. The first — and only — TR1 prototype was shown at the British Earls Court Motor Show in October 1952. Since then, more than a quarter of a million production cars, in six major series, have been built. The current TR7, already burgeoning into several versions, looks like being the most popular of all.

Even so, all over the world there is a great deal of confusion about the TR's history and development. Many thousands of cars — new, not-so-new and classic — are loved and preserved by Triumph enthusiasts, often against a background of ignorance. The factory, perforce, has dropped its service and technical back-up of the older TRs.

This means that many owners are not sure about their cars' originality — which models should have what fittings, what items were standard and what fittings might not be accurate, or what cars are the most rare and which the least notable. This book, I hope, will clear up all the doubts.

It is, quite simply, a book of facts. From July 1953, when the first production TR2 was built, to late 1977, when the latest engine and equipment options are being added to the TR7, I try to lead the TR owner through a minefield of model changes, major up-dates, important improvements and cross-links with other Triumphs. There is very little space, though, for me to explore the philosophy which has inspired the TRs, or the reasoning behind some of the hard-to-understand changes.

I hope it will also settle the history of the various competition programmes — the events, the successes and the cars — the evolution of the prototypes (many later sold off to private customers) and the identity of special machines which evolved from the standard product.

For the enthusiasts and historians, perhaps the most important parts of the book are the Appendices. All these facts, provided after much diligent research by the Triumph factory, show how many of each TR model were built, when each model was being built, and what were their principal features.

Important mid-model junctions — the introduction of TR3 disc brakes, and the onset of stiffer North American anti-emission legislation on the TR6 are just two examples — make abundantly clear the evolution of these very fine cars.

It is encouraging, too, to think that this book will eventually go out-of-date, and that with so many TR7s being sold, and so many interesting future TR developments already in the pipeline, an updated edition some time in the future seems inevitable — or so my publisher assures me!

GRAHAM ROBSON

November 1977

Introduction to Second Edition

For the 1981 reprint of this book, I have been able to update the information and the unfolding saga of the TR7 and TR8 models, while bringing the competition record up to date and correcting one or two doubtful points about earlier models. In spite of the continuing controversy which surrounds the TR7/TR8 family, including the threat to withdraw it from production, at least temporarily, in the closing months of 1981, it should be noted that it is already the most numerous of all the TRs built in the last three decades.

GRAHAM ROBSON

May 1981

CHAPTER 1

Ancestors and parentage

1800 and 2000, TRX and TR1

When Standard-Triumph settled down to design a 2-litre sports car in 1952 they were not hampered by any hidebound sports car traditions. The Triumph marque had been owned by Standard since 1945, though there had been Triumph cars since 1923. Since the change in ownership, following World War Two, no other two-seater Triumph had yet been sold.

Between the wars, and most prominently in the 1930s, there had been some fine sporting Triumphs, but the old company's financial problems meant that they were never promoted with great vigour. After the war, it was Sir John Black of Standard who was determined to make much of the notable name.

The first post-war Triumphs, announced in 1946, used Flying Standard engines, transmissions and suspensions in a cheap-to-tool tubular frame, topped by alloy-panelled body-shells. The 1800 Town and Country Saloon had bodies by Mulliners of Birmingham, while the 1800 Roadster was bodied at the Standard factory.

The 1800 was sporting, but not a sports car. It carried over the pre-war Triumph feature of a dickey seat (or rumble seat if you are American), had a convertible hood and three-abreast bench seating. The 1,776cc engine was shared with Jaguar's 1½-litre range, and it had a steering-column gear change. Later in the run, both the Saloon and the Roadster were given the 2,088cc wet-liner Standard Vanguard engine, gearbox and transmission. The saloon also inherited a long-wheelbase version of the Vanguard's box-sectio chassis frame (and carried on, so equipped, until 1955), though the Roadster kept its tubular frame until it went out of production at the end of 1949.

Standard-Triumph were sufficiently encouraged by the sales of their 1800 and 2000 Roadsters (4,500 built in four years) to allow their chief body engineer, Walter Belgrove, to design a replacement. His brief was that though he should use unmodified Standard Vanguard chassis and mechanical components, his body theme could be unrestricted. Unlike the old Roadsters, the new car had an up-to-the-minute and fully-equipped body style in double-skinned light-alloy, without a dickey seat, and with electro-hydraulic operation of such items as the foldaway hood, the seat adjustment and the hide-away headlamps.

The TRX, as it was always known, was very much of a personal statement of modern styling — so much so that Walter Belgrove was allowed to add a monogrammed 'B' badge to the front wings behind the wheel-arches. It was much more of a touring car than a sporting machine, and would have been expensive to produce. A combination of two things — adverse public reaction and Standard's preoccupation with other new and potentially-profitable models — meant that the TRX was never put into production. Three prototypes were finished in 1950, and two of them survive to this day.

TRX was finally cancelled during 1951, but by the beginning of 1952 Sir John Black was ready to look at sporting Triumphs once again. This time he was motivated by Standard's failure to take over the tiny Morgan company, and was jealous of the success of MG's TD from Abingdon, and of Jaguar's XK120 from the other side of Coventry.

The real TR story, therefore, begins in the first weeks of 1952, though the successful TR2s and TR3s built in such profusion in the 1950s did not have much in common with the original concept. 'The Triumph Sports Car', as it was catalogued at the

Standard-Triumph's first post-war sporting car was the 1800 Roadster, announced in March 1946. It had a tubular chassis frame and a light-alloy coachbuilt body. There was normally two or three-abreast seating, but a hinged panel behind the hood recess revealed a double 'dickey' seat as well. Access to the dickey was over the tail — note the foot pad on the corner of the rear bumper. The mechanical components were all taken from existing Flying Standards, except that the engine was a rather special overhead-valve unit shared with the '1½ Litre' Jaguar of the day. The 1800 was re-engined in 1948, becoming the 2000 Roadster. A total of 4,500 Roadsters were built from 1946 to the end of 1949.

1952 Motor Show (it only became known as the TR1 in later years and was never coded as such in the factory), was a much simpler and more basic machine.

For one thing, its body was to be restricted to severe tooling-cost limits, and for another the designers, led by Harry Webster, were being pressured to use as many existing or even obsolete Standard-Triumph parts as possible. This meant that in the original concept a Flying Standard Nine chassis frame (obsolete for some years) was to form the basis. Possible sales were projected at no more than 500 a year, and there just happened to be several hundred such frames in existence . . .

Even before the first prototype TR1 was built it was obvious that the frame was torsionally and longitudinally weak. In time for that first showing, therefore, a new frame was produced, and a frantic buildup was completed just in time for the October announcement. The new frame, however, carried over the first ideas — it had a Triumph Mayflower (of 1949 vintage) front suspension, which was independent with coil springs and wishbones, and the rear axle was that of the Mayflower but with slightly reduced track.

The engine was a slightly-modified Standard Vanguard unit, with twin 1½in SU carburettors, and with 83mm cylinder bore

Facia of the TRX showing definite Standard Vanguard influence. Walter Belgrove had wanted this car to have circular dials, but the finished product was not as pure nor as sporting as he had originally intended in 1948-49. There was only a three-speed gearbox, and the seat was a full-width bench.

Engine bay of the TRX, showing the bonnet lifting from the side rather than from front or rear. The twin-SU carburettor installation can be seen, but even an enthusiast may not realise that the carbs are on the wrong side. This TRX prototype was fitted with a one-off cylinder-head in which the inlet manifolding was on the left. On all production Vanguard/TR installations, of course, the carburettors are on the right.

To replace the 2000 Roadster Triumph considered this 'New Roadster', which was Walter Belgrove's personal design creation. The chassis and running gear were all lifted direct from the Standard Vanguard, except that the engine was mildly tuned and equipped with twin SU carburettors. In this respect the engine was a direct ancestor of that of the TR2, though in this application it was still of 2,088cc capacity. The body-shell was touring rather than sporting, with light-alloy double-skinned panelling, and electro-hydraulic operation of the headlamps, foldaway hood and seat adjustment. The headlamps were behind panels in the wings and, as with the 1800/2000 Roadster, there was a steering column gear-change. It was always coded TRX.

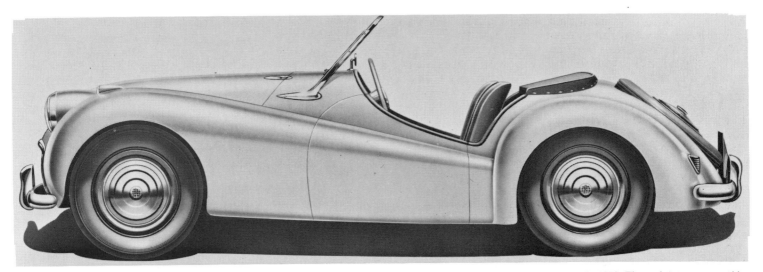

An original styling sketch by Walter Belgrove of his design for the new '20TS' Triumph Sports Car, a study completed early in 1952. The style was governed by the extremely tight limit on capital available for body tooling (almost every panel was restricted to single-curvature sections). The short tail styling was partly influenced by the short chassis frame under it — the pre-war Flying Standard Nine frame was the original choice.

The very first TR prototype chassis frame revealed in a September 1952 photograph never previously published. The frame has already progressed some way from the Flying Standard origins, but is nothing like as sturdy as the TR2 frame would soon become.

Even though the gearbox had four forward speeds, the original concept was to have a short, direct-acting gear-lever without the benefit of a remote-control linkage.

wet liners to bring the capacity just under the 2-litre limit for sporting purposes. The gearbox was very similar to the Vanguard design, but had four speeds (no synchromesh on first gear) and a remote control from a stubby little gear lever. The very first rolling chassis had a direct-action lever, but this was never seen in public.

Walter Belgrove styled the open two-seater body. Sir John Black had told him that it "could look as traditional as the MG or Morgan" if he wished it, but Belgrove chose a cobby little modern shape, with simple and — as he called it — 'undertooled' panels. It looked much the same as the production cars which followed it, except from the tail where there was a short sweep down from the seats and an exposed spare wheel and a filler neck for the fuel tank which protruded through the middle of the spare-wheel fixings. The tank, incidentally, held 12 gallons, but was a different shape and in a different location from the production cars — it was slung behind, rather than above, the back axle.

The story of the TR1's transformation into the legendary TR2 is well-known. It revolves round a chassis redesign during the winter of 1952-53; the building of three new prototypes and the scrapping of the original; a crash programme of development and proving carried out by Ken Richardson (who had been hired from BRM to do precisely that job); and a power-tuning exercise which eventually produced the dead-reliable 90bhp at 4,800rpm compared with the TR1's 75bhp at 4,500rpm.

In the process, the car's maximum speed went up from 90mph to about 105mph, and its performance capability was splendidly demonstrated on the Jabbeke motorway in Belgium in the early morning of May 20, 1953, when it was taken on a series of two-way runs through a flying kilometre, in three states of trim, to record the following mean speeds:

Speed trim (undershield, metal tonneau, no screen or hood): 124.9mph

Touring trim (screen erect, hood and sidescreens, but undershield in place), using overdrive: 114.9mph

Touring trim (as above), without overdrive: 109.0mph

Progress, in redesign, proving, and in the original somewhat temporary production tooling, was so rapid that the car which had been revealed as a 'first thoughts' TR1 in October 1952 was ready for small-scale production by the summer of 1953.

Historians and collectors will want to know the details of the five prototypes built in 1952 and 1953. These were as follows:

Triumph experimental chassis number	Year built	Registration number	Comments
X505	1952	Not registered	The only TR1 built, later scrapped.
X508	1953 January	MWK950	First prototype TR2, left-hand drive.
X519	1953 March	MVC575	Second prototype TR2, left-hand drive: the Jabbeke run car.
X516	1953 Autumn	ORW666	Third prototype TR2, right-hand drive.
X509	1953	Not listed	Development/proving of 4.1 axle ratio.

The one and only TR1, exhibited at Earls Court in October 1952. From this view the only details soon to be changed were the wing-top side lamps, which would be moved, the over-riders would be simplified, and the hood stowage would be tidied-up.

Three-quarters rear view of the unique TR1 showing the bob-tail style with the exposed spare wheel. The fuel tank filler cap is housed in the middle of the spare wheel clamp. The number plate was intended to stand proud of the bodywork, as is obvious from this view. The major visual change from TR1 prototype to TR2 production car was that the tail was lengthened and made more angular. It would also incorporate a luggage boot — the TR1 had none.

Ken Richardson in the left-hand-drive TR2 prototype, actually the second TR2 to be built and the third TR of all, as used for the highspeed runs at Jabbeke, in Belgium, in May 1953. The body shape has taken its definitive production form, with the addition of a special non-standard undershield, and the rear wheel-arch spats which were listed as a performance option, but apparently were never made available to the public. The bonnet badge is also unique — the well-loved TR2 insignia would replace it from the start of series production. The tonneau cover on MVC 575 was of metal and purely for streamlining purposes. In this guise it achieved a two-way 124mph.

CHAPTER 2

The classic TR — 1953 to 1962

TR2, TR3, TR3A and TR3B

The pace of events was extraordinary. Design and styling had begun earlier in 1952, but the unique TR1 was assembled in a mere eight weeks — from August to October 1952. A redesign, both of the chassis and of the body styling and engineering, was completed in a matter of weeks. Sir John Black took the stub-tailed TR1 to the United States in February 1953, but the first proper TR2 was revealed at the Geneva Motor Show in March. That car, in fact, became MVC 575 and was used for the Jabbeke speed runs.

For the first few months, Triumph would look after chassis frame assembly themselves (from Commission Number TS1401 it would be sourced from Sankeys), while the body-shells would be supplied from the Mulliners Ltd Birmingham factory which also built the razor-edge Triumph Renown bodies.

To satisfy themselves that all the tooled-up bits and pieces fitted together properly, the experimental department at Banner Lane, Coventry, actually assembled the first two production cars. TS1LO was a white left-hand-drive car sent out to Canada for the Automobile Show, while TS2 was a white right-hand-drive machine sent to Ireland for the Dublin Motor Show. Both these cars were shipped in July 1953.

Both, incidentally, are still alive and well, the one in Canada, and the ex-Dublin car now being owned by Keith Read, who is Motoring Correspondent of the *Coventry Evening Telegraph.*

The first true production car rolled off the assembly line at Canley in August 1953, immediately after the factory's summer shut-down, but for several months the build rate was very low. Just on 250 cars were built before the beginning of 1954, of which a mere 50 stayed in Britain. These 50, incidentally, went to

carefully selected dealers, most of whom were ready to use their cars in rallies and other competitions as soon as possible, where the hoped-for success would bring a publicity boost. Quite a few of these early cars, too, were registered in Coventry before delivery, which explains why such a large proportion of the 1954 competition TR2s appear to be 'works' team cars!

The early TR2s were in great demand, for several reasons, which are best summed up as low price, high performance, low running costs and ready availability. Anyone lucky enough to take delivery of a 1953 TR2 paid only £555 (before tax), but from January 1954 the price was raised to £595 and from October 1954 it jumped again to £625. At any one of these prices, however, the TR2 was an obvious bargain. Its competitors were the MG TF (£550 — and with much less performance), the Morgan Plus 4 (£585 with the TR2 engine), the Jowett Jupiter (£725 — just about to disappear from the market), the Austin-Healey 100 (£750), and the Jaguar XK120 (£1,130).

Of all this competition, the XK120 was much faster, but in a completely different market, while the more expensive Austin-Healey had a 2.7-litre engine and was too low-slung to be versatile; both incidentally, were in extremely short supply in Britain. On a car-for-car basis, the TR2 was quite unrivalled, and its sporting achievements in the next few years would prove this conclusively.

Once properly in production from the beginning of 1954, TR2s began to dominate the British market. It was Triumph's policy at that stage that a reasonable proportion of the cars should stay at home. On the other hand only about 1,500 MGs had been sold in Britain in 1953, very few Morgans were being made at all, and all

Rear suspension and axle of the TR2 display chassis, showing the Mayflower-based back-axle assembly. That original Burgess exhaust silencer allowed a very fruity note to get through to the outside world, especially under hard acceleration. There was a particularly raucous 'bark' at about 2,500rpm. Note the bump straps above the axle-tube — lack of wheel movement was always a problem with the live-axle TRs. However, the lack of rebound movement (the chassis side-members limited this severely) gave rise to the TR2/3/4 characteristic side-skip on bumpy roads. The damper bracketry was usually much-stiffened on competition cars, and larger lever-arm dampers were often used.

The definitive TR2 chassis in show-prepared form. This is a left-hand-drive example, and the hydraulic master cylinders and pedals are being supported in mid-air by a display bracket.

Nose details of the production TR2 chassis with the original water outlet from the cylinder-head, but with a blanking plate in place of the filler cap. At this stage, too, the front brakes were 10-inch Lockheeds while the rears were 9-inch.

This is an historic picture — it shows the first redesigned chassis — effectively TR2 instead of TR1 — to be completed early in 1953. All the elements of the production version are now present, including the remote-control gear-change. Note, however, that the gear-lever knob is non-standard (it appears to be from the still-secret Standard Eight), and that the later centre cruciform stiffeners and the stronger rear damper mountings have yet to be developed.

19

but about 100 XK120s were being exported every year.

Almost immediately the list of optional equipment began to proliferate. A large proportion of the cars were fitted with overdrive — at first only applicable to top gear but later to top, third and second gears — and many were also fitted with centre-lock wire wheels. A TR restorer could get very confused about wire wheels, for although all types seem to fit the same splines, in the future they would variously have 48-spoke, 60-spoke or even occasionally 72-spoke (TR6) patterns, with a whole variety of finishes including body paint, silver paint, bright chrome, dull chrome . . .

The very early cars suffered a very noisy exhaust system, with a resonant period at about 2,500rpm. It was something in which the 'cowboys' revelled, but the factory soon realized the embarrassment and revised the silencing arrangements.

Reliability and performance were never problematical, but braking and roadholding were! Disc brakes were not available on any production car at this stage, and the Lockheed drum system provided on the TR2 had the double vices of too much front-wheel braking and a tendency to grab and/or fade when used really hard. About the roadholding, there was little to be done, as the problem centred around limited rear-axle movement (particularly rebound movement — the axle came down firmly on the chassis side-member, after which the inside wheel tended to lift) and the rather primitive tyres with which cars of the TR's price tended to be equipped in those days.

The first true advance in tyres came when Michelin X covers were offered on TR3s. These undoubtedly improved the tyre life, and also the grip in most conditions, but as the early Xs has something of a reputation for rapid breakaway in wet conditions the TR owner was presented with a new idiosyncracy to learn.

All this, of course, was minor compared with the great virtues of effortless performance, great reliability, and what turned out to be an astonishing fuel-economy potential. This last feature was, of course, partly due to the high gearing, the light weight and the reasonable aerodynamics, but it was also due to a lucky combination of engine breathing, valve timing and carburettor settings on those early cars. TR2s could be relied on for well over 30mpg, perhaps even over 35mpg, in normal (and that meant fast motoring) use. However, each time the design was changed to give more power the economy potential dropped a little; only the original engines with 1½in SU carburettors gave really outstanding figures.

The best, and most extreme, example was when Richard Bensted-Smith, of *The Motor*, achieved 71mpg in a no-holds-barred run to win the Mobilgas Economy Run.

Note, too, that at Le Mans in 1954 the TR2 completed the 24-hour race at 74.71mph and 34.68mpg.

In the autumn of 1954 a whole series of improvements were phased in, not all at the same Commission point, which makes it a bit confusing for historians. Two body changes which were most obvious and most desirable were the fitting of 'short' doors, and the optional glass-fibre hardtop. The fitting of fixed sills under the doors both stiffened the body-shell and allowed the doors to be opened easily alongside high kerbs (the TR2 was *that* low). The hardtop was equally valuable for the not-so-young customer who didn't want the wind in his hair, and for the rally drivers who wanted a bit of comfort while going about their craft.

Equally important was that the braking system had been re-worked. Although Lockheed drums were still specified, the rear drums had been increased to the same size as the fronts and the balance was much improved. That change, incidentally, came in from TS5443, while the short doors date from TS4002, and the second-third-top overdrive control from TS6266. There is no point in quoting an introduction point for hardtops as these could be, and often were, later fitted to earlier TR2s than the October 1954 model.

Sales and production continued to expand, but from October 1955 the TR2 was dropped in favour of the TR3. This change, in fact, was more in name than in nature, and caused very little aggravation to the Canley production lines. TS8636 was the last of the TR2s and TS8637 the first of the TR3s. The important mechanical changes were the fitting of an uprated engine, quoted at 95bhp instead of 90bhp — the extra power being found through enlarged inlet ports and larger 1¾in SU carburettors — and the addition of a 4.1 axle-ratio option.

An 'egg-box' radiator grille was added for decorative purposes, with stainless steel beading along the wing/body-shell joints, while it was now possible to order an 'occasional' rear seat. Surprisingly, a good many people did just that, although they must have had extra passengers with very strange anatomy as legroom was nil unless the front seats were pushed well forward.

The nearly-completed interior of the first left-hand drive TR2 prototype, pictured in the spring of 1953. The simple and very easily read instruments and the logical layout of minor controls would be a feature of the TRs right from the start. The knob on the far left of the panel, almost hidden by the wheel rim, actuates the optional overdrive.

21

One of the first production-line TR2s, with Ken Richardson at the wheel. This is the original 1953-54 model, complete with full-depth doors, 'globe' badges on the wheel trims and the TR2 'shield' badge on the nose. Note the very simple over-riders, and compare details with TR1 pictures shown in Chapter 1.

Well-loved view of the classic TR2 with its very practical tail. The boot-lid was locked or unlocked by a special key, the locks being covered by small chrome escutcheons near the rear corners of the lid. The same locking arrangements served to hold the spare wheel cover panel in place. The tail-lamps with their 'hung on' reflectors were discarded for the better-known integrated design late in 1954.

Shortly after the TR3's introduction — within weeks, in fact — the company embarked on a very confusing series of engine changes. The 1955 Le Mans team cars had tried an improved type of cylinder-head, different enough to be given its special part number, and this was now progressively phased in for the TR3. The first engine so fitted was TS9350E, but at TS12606E a further change was made.

This time the cylinder-head, with yet another part number and yet another inlet manifold to suit, was what is now known as the 'high-port' head, and combined the best features of the original TR2 head and the 'Le Mans' head. Fair enough, but the real confusion is that from TS12606E to TS13051E there was no logic as to which combination would be found when the engine was finally fitted to the car!

This pantomime persisted at Canley from the end of 1955 to midsummer 1956. Almost coincident, but not quite, with the next major up-date of the TR3s, the engine specification settled down, and all subsequent four-cylinder TR engines used versions of the 'high-port' cylinder-head, until the last was built in 1967.

In August 1956, immediately after the resumption of manufacture following the summer holiday shut-down, the TR3 was greatly improved. The sensational adoption of Girling front-wheel disc brakes made the headlines, but there was more to it than this. All TR collectors will want to remember the Commission Number TS13046, the first of the revised cars.

When the Lockheed drum-brake system was discarded and the Girling system substituted for it, the rear drums were kept at the same size as before — 10in diameter with shoes 2¼in wide. Let us be quite clear about this — the TR3 was the very first British series-production car to have disc brakes as standard equipment, and after the French Citroen DS19 it was the second series-production car in Europe.

Jensen owners make much of the fact that the 541 was given Dunlop disc brakes to all four wheels at the same time — in fact the Triumph made their announcement weeks before Jensen and were already building cars at the rate of at least 150 to 200 every week, while Jensen might make two cars (or if it was a good period three cars) in a week.

Almost as important, as any TR2/TR3 owner with the earlier type will assure you, was the fitment, from the same Commission Number, of a stronger Phase III Vanguard-type rear axle. This,

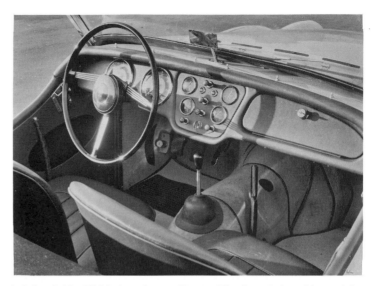

Left-hand-drive TR2 facia and control layout. The dip-switch position and the recessed trim panel to allow foot room are clearly visible.

though it used the same crownwheel and pinion sets and the differential from earlier TRs, was different in many respects. There were taper roller bearings in place of ball bearings to support the sturdier half-shafts, and completely redesigned hubs to suit the new 10in Girling rear brakes. Incidentally, to show that logic was something in short supply at Standard-Triumph in the mid-1950s, the rear axle adopted for this TR3 had originally been designed for the 51in track Vanguard III, which had Lockheed drums.

In the meantime, the factory had decided to make available a 'GT' car kit. This looked very minor on the surface, and so it was, as it only involved the use of a steel instead of a glass-fibre hardtop, and the addition of exterior door handles (which obviated the owner having to wriggle his arm through the hinged side-curtain to get at the interior release). However, it had been done for the benefit of Ken Richardson's works competition department, so that they could pick and choose between their categories — Sports or Grand Touring. These kits had been blooded on the 1956 Alpine Rally, where the team cars had been

The first important TR2 development changes came in the autumn of 1954, and most are obvious from this side view. Structurally the most significant was that the door depth was decreased and a fixed sill was added between the front and rear quarters. This allowed the doors to be opened more readily over high kerbs. The new tail-lamps can be seen in profile. Among the new options, which would become very popular indeed, were the glass-fibre hardtop (complete with the new sliding sidescreens). Not as obvious, but just as valuable, were the bigger 10-inch rear brakes and the optional telescopic steering column.

As shown on the book's dust cover, there is a striking contrast between a TR2 of 1954-55 and the latest TR7s.

After just two years of TR production the TR3 arrived. Visually there were few changes, the most noticeable being the addition of the 'egg crate' grille and the change from 'TR2' to 'TR3' on the nose badge. The engine's power was increased by 5bhp, as important improvements continued to be made to the unburstable 1,991cc engine.

A TR3 with a history — and a difference. This was a 1956 model, kitted out by Ken Richardson with a metal hardtop and other details so that it could qualify as a Grand Touring instead of a sports car. It was subsequently used by Richardson, without success, in the 1956 Alpine Rally (where five other TR3s won *Coupes des Alpes*), and was raced (and crashed!) by Nancy Mitchell in the 1957 Mille Miglia. In all other respects, however, SHP 520, when new, was a typical example of the TR3.

The TR3 engine, of 1,991cc, laid out for inspection. The four-bladed fan can be seen on the nose of the crankshaft and the later type of hot water outlet from the cylinder-head is clearly shown.

The interior of a 1956 TR3. The pull-out overdrive switch can just be seen to the right of the rev counter.

A very occasional rear seat was optional on TR3s (and later, of course, this feature continued on TR3As). This shot was taken with the front seats adjusted well forward; in truth there was very little leg-room in the back, and even less head-room with hood or hardtop erect.

enormously successful.

Sales and production of TR3s were now accelerating rapidly, as a study of Commission Numbers proves. Only 8,628 TR2s were built between July 1953 and October 1955 — an average of about 300 cars a month — while 13,378 TR3s would be built from October 1955 to the summer of 1957 — about twice the rate for TR2s. A study of registrations shows that the TR's export performance was continuing to improve, and the result was a squeeze on deliveries at home.

This was good enough, and was already embarrassing BMC's MG factory, but there was more to come. In the summer of 1957, quite unknown to the British motoring press and without any fuss from Triumph, a modified type of TR3 began to flow down the Canley lines. This was the legendary TR3A, though I must confirm at once that the car was never *officially* known as the TR3A by Triumph's sales staff, at least not at first, but eventually even they bowed to popular opinion and the name with which it was dubbed. Certainly the car was never badged — front or rear — as anything but a TR3.

Mechanically there was nothing to distinguish a TR3A from a TR3. The engine's power output had risen officially to 100bhp at 5,000rpm in the autumn of 1956, this figure signalling the final and complete adoption of the 'high-port' cylinder-head. All the mechanical options applicable to the previous model remained available.

Externally, the obvious difference was the new nose panel, which incorporated a full-width grille and had the headlamps slightly recessed into the sloping sheet metal (TR2s and TR3s had slightly protruding headlamps); the grille also housed the side lamp/indicator lenses, previously mounted in the nose at each side of the grille.

The exterior door handles previously special to the 'GT' kit were standardized, and similarly lockable handles were fitted to the boot-lid.

This important change occurred at TS22014, and several thousand cars were delivered to the United States before the TR3A was released for the rest of the world at the very beginning of 1958. In Britain the basic price crept up to £699, compared with £680 for the last of the TR3s.

Production now really rocketed upwards, and many more TR3As were sold — over 58,000 — than any other 'classic' TR. At

The most obvious change from TR3 to TR3A was in the fitting of this full-width radiator grille. The entire front panel was changed, with headlamps slightly recessed instead of slightly protruding. Note, however, that the badge was never altered; all TR3As and TR3Bs were equipped with the same familiar 'TR3' badge.

its peak in 1960 nearly 2,000 cars were built in a month and the TR3A carried on without important visible changes until 1961 and the release of the TR4.

Under the skin, however, development changes continued to be made. In the main, these were to improve reliability and durability, but two changes were of particular importance. From TS56378 (in the winter of 1959-60) a completely revised braking system was introduced. This involved the use of Girling 'split B' disc-brake callipers, while at approximately the same time the rear brake drums were reduced in size to 9in diameter by 1¾in shoe width. This installation, incidentally, would be used by the first batch of TR4s in 1961-62.

From TS60001, too, the body-shell was substantially retooled, especially around the cockpit/screen/hood fixings area. Nothing was visible from outside the car. However, behind the seats there

The TR3A went into production in the summer of 1957, and was sold exclusively in the United States until January 1958, when it was offered to the rest of the world. Among the improvements were the new frontal styling, the engine power boosted to 100bhp, and the fitment of lockable exterior door handles, along with lockable handles for opening the boot lid. Seats and trim were also improved.

The TR3A's facia and instruments, the layout unchanged from earlier models but with better trim arrangements. The radio, of course, was an extra fitting. The overdrive switch (visible by the spoke of the steering wheel) was of the tumbler variety. The side carpets are not yet installed in this new car.

Complete engine/gearbox/overdrive assembly ready for installing into a TR3A. Visually this assembly changed very little from 1953 to 1962.

Above: Rear-end detail of the first production TR2, showing the separate spare wheel stowage and the cover panel along with the simple but spacious boot. The reflector arrangement, in fact, is non-standard. Above right: The first true left-hand-drive TR2 prototype, still with its unique bonnet badge. The engine was a snug fit under the bonnet, but there was enough space for maintenance and repairs.

The nose of an early track-built TR2, showing the guide hole for the starting handle and the simple protective mesh at the back of the intake ducting.

was a flat platform, instead of the sloping panel, and this meant that occasional-seating arrangements had to be revised. The windscreen became mounted by proper bolts, bonnet and boot-lid hinge mountings were fixed to slightly raised platforms in the pressings, and the electrical system went over completely to Lucas snap connectors.

This was probably done due to the original tools wearing out (nobody, after all, could have forecast in 1953, when the tools were laid down, that the TR2 and its derivatives would still be selling strongly seven years later), and it explains why no obvious styling or engineering changes were included at the same time.

In the meantime, Ken Richardson's rallying team had proved the worth of the 86mm bore, 2,138cc engine conversion kit, which allowed them more torque (if little more power) in 2,500cc competition classes, and from 1959 this had been offered as an option along with many other existing items.

Many owners converted their own engines, as it was very simply done. The cylinder barrels, after all, were slip-fit 'wet' liners, so one new set of liners and the appropriate pistons and rings provided an isntant and none-too-expensive performance conversion. Figures for the number of engines or kits so supplied do not exist at Triumph any more, so only a speculation can be made of their frequency, but many TR3As were converted retrospectively by their first or even a subsequent owner.

Though the TR3A, in the end, can be judged enormously successful, there is little doubt that it was over-produced by Standard-Triumph. By the spring of 1961, with the company deep in financial trouble and about to be taken over by Leyland Motors, production had fallen dramatically, and during the summer months (before the TR4 was launched) there was a hiatus when TR3A build was virtually stopped. Even so, as a mass-production British sports car it was only then being outsold by the MGA, and then only by a tiny margin.

The TR4 and its derivatives must be described in the next chapter, but its influence was felt even by the TR3A. When the North American dealer chain was shown the TR4, they expressed the opinion that it was too smooth and too grown-up for all their TR customers. Accordingly they demanded, and Triumph agreed to supply, a further batch of 'classic' TRs. Thus the near-mythical TR3B was briefly born, and put into production in 1962.

As with the TR3A, the TR3B as a *model* name didn't officially exist. Certainly a TR3B looks identical to a TR3A, and both are badged as plain TR3s. In fact just 3,331 of these cars were built, their bodies being constructed by the Forward Radiator Company, from existing tools shipped to them from Mulliners Ltd, who had built all the other TRs. (Just to confuse matters further, TR4s and all subsequent cars of that family would be built by Standard-Triumph Liverpool, yet another body factory!)

The first 500 TR3Bs were in the TSF Commission Number series, and had 1,991cc engines. The other TR3Bs were all in the TCF series and had 2,138cc engines. Both types had the TR4 all-synchromesh gearbox. Because of their rarity value, and because the chassis/engine/transmission combination is so nice, the 'TCF' TR3Bs are very desirable. Note that a few TSFs may have had non-TR4 gearboxes.

By then, however, this particular TR philosophy was out-of-date. The TR4, with its smoother, more modern and considerably more refined coachwork, had arrived. The Leyland Motors takeover marked a watershed in the affairs of the TR, for without their arrival the Standard-Triumph combine might have collapsed financially, and after it the accent on TRs was inclined to comfort rather than outright sports-car behaviour, as will be explained in the next chapter.

CHAPTER 3

The TR in transition — 1961 to 1967

TR4 and TR4A

The original and very successful TR2 formula reigned for eight years, but between 1961 and 1967 there was a complete design revolution. This occurred in three distinct moves — an entirely new body-shell in 1961, an advanced new chassis and suspension in 1965, and finally an ultra-modern engine in 1967. In those six years, without showing any obvious strains, the overall Triumph TR philosophy was turned on its head. The rugged and simple car of the 1950s became a smooth and sophisticated machine for the 1970s.

With the TR3A safely launched, Triumph looked at several ways to restyle the TR series. They made more than one false start, described in some detail in Chapter 7. The 'Zest' project, which finally matured in 1961, became the new TR4. Its new body style was the work of Triumph's Italian consultant Giovanni Michelotti.

The TR4 is often called a TR3A with a new body, but that is an injustice to the real and very worthwhile mechanical changes — principally the wide tracks, the rack-and-pinion steering, the all-synchromesh gearbox and the standardization of the 86mm bore engine.

Mechanically, however, the TR4 *was* much as before. Front and rear tracks were increased to 49in and 48in, and the only chassis frame changes needed to accommodate this were the stiffening-up of the front end, the repositioning of the front suspension towers and extra members alongside the front of the main side-members; front suspension members and geometry were — for the time being at least — unchanged.

At the same time the old TR2/3/3A/3B cam-and-lever steering was discarded, and rack-and-pinion steering (with a steering column having much in common with that of the Triumph Herald) was fitted instead. The rack slotted neatly into place behind the radiator and ahead of the engine. At the rear, the extra track was achieved simply by having an axle with lengthened tubes and half-shafts; leaf spring fixings to the chassis were not affected.

It is possible, incidentally, to put this new chassis under the old TR2/3/3A/3B body-shell, but the wings ought to be reprofiled to give the same amount of splash cover to the tyres.

The other principal mechanical changes were to the engine and gearbox. The engine standardized was the 86mm by 92mm, 2,138cc unit previously optional on TR3As and standard on 'TCF' TR3Bs. The old 1,991cc unit remained as a no-cost option throughout the life of the TR4, but few were actually ordered. In all major respects, however, neither engine was altered; the power of the 2,138cc version was quoted as 100bhp *nett*, a different and more conservative measurement than that used for previous TRs.

The gearbox, though looking similar to the familiar TR3A unit, was very different internally. It is far too easy to say that for the first time bottom gear was synchronized and leave it at that. Although the top, third and second gear ratios were all unchanged inside the box, and some parts had been carried over from TR3A to TR4, it is quite impossible for a TR3A box to be converted to TR4 specification as the gearbox casing itself is new.

The biggest changes, however, were in the body style. Whereas the old TR3A shell had been built in Birmingham, at the Triumph-owned Mulliners (and finally the Forward Radiator) factories, the TR4 shell was pressed and assembled at the new Standard-Triumph Liverpool plant, in Speke. TR enthusiasts

The dramatically new shape of the 1961 TR4, styled by Michelotti, and with a shell built in Triumph's own body plant at Liverpool. Under the skin much of the legendary TR3/TR3A chassis was retained. Among the obvious features in this view is the full-width bonnet, which hinged at the nose, the low build necessitating a bonnet bulge over the dashpots of the SU carburettors, and the more fully integrated windscreen.

there had to be a 'power bulge' above the dashpots of the SU carburettors to give clearance when they were rocking about on engine mountings. This bulge, incidentally, stayed in place throughout the life of the TR5/TR250 cars, even though the lower six-cylinder engines didn't need it any more.

The most important development of all was that there was no longer a cutaway for the driver's elbow, and no side screens; wind-up windows were provided instead. There was a completely new facia, but the instruments, their styling and their function, were those of the old TRs. Even the seats were basically those introduced for the TR3A in 1957-58.

The boot space was larger than before, mainly due to the fact that the rear deck didn't slope like that of the older TRs. That was good news. The bad news was that the spare wheel no longer lived in a compartment of its own. It was still slung between the rear chassis side rails, but access was from the boot itself. In the event of a puncture, any luggage in the boot had first to be removed before the spare wheel could be taken out of the well.

All the familiar TR options — like overdrive, an optional axle ratio, or wire wheels — were continued, as was the hardtop, but this was completely different in design, and incorporated the still-unique 'Surrey top' feature.

The TR4 hardtop came in two pieces. At the rear, a stout light-alloy casting doubled as a surround for the hardtop's rear window, and as a roll-over bar in case of accident. Bridging the gap between this member and the windscreen header rail was a pressed-steel roof member which bolted into place. If the customer wished, he could also order the 'Surrey top', which was a vinyl roof panel supported by a light frame.

Among the other advances were the safety-collapse feature for the steering column, the fitting of a fresh-air heater and the provision of fresh-air vents at each end of the facia, something which pre-dated the much-publicized Ford Cortina layout by three whole years. There was provision for a brake servo to be added (it lived between the right-side inner wheel-arch and the scuttle panel).

The TR4 moved smoothly into production in the autumn of 1961, and sold well right from the start. Although it was somewhat heavier than the TR3A, its uprated engine allowed much the same performance to be maintained, and the sychronized first gear was a definite boon for traffic jam

must have seen the shells being transported, up to 12 at a time in specially built transporter trucks, from Liverpool to Coventry, where final assembly took place.

The new shell, like the old, was of pressed steel, but was in a full-width style, whereas the TR2/3/3A/3B body had sported almost separate wings. The grille was full-width, but so was the bonnet. Unlike that of the old shell, the TR4's bonnet hinged at the front, and it was so closely shaped around the engine that

The hoods over the headlamps are clearly seen in this three-quarter view. The full-width style, with an almost straight-through waistline, allowed wind-up door window glasses to be specified. As before, wire wheels were options.

Boot and spare wheel stowage arrangements of the TR4. Whereas spare wheel access had been separate on the TR2/3/3A series, on the TR4 and subsequent models the wheel was inside the boot under a cover. Even so, there was much more luggage space than before.

The TR4's facia and instruments, showing an 'under-sold' feature — the face-level ventilation. Ford were to make much of this with their 1965-model Cortinas, whereas Triumph had this system in 1961. On the TR4 the steering-column engineering was shared with the Heralds and (later) the Vitesses, one result of which was that the overdrive control was on the column. A fresh-air heater was now specified, while the steering wheel was new.

Above: The original TR4 seats were as used by the TR3A. There was marginally more space in the rear than before, and an 'occasional' seat was optional. Seat belt mountings — seen on the inner wheel arches — were now specified.
Above right: The TR4 in chassis form. The only obvious changes were that rack-and-pinion steering had been added — the rack can be seen behind the radiator shell — and both front and rear tracks had been increased by four inches. Note, too, the additional exhaust silencer behind the rear-axle line.

Front suspension details of an early-type TR4, complete with rack-and-pinion steering, but with TR3A wishbones and other components. This is a left-hand-drive chassis, and the steering column has yet to be fitted to the rack. There is still a radiator hole to allow a starting handle to be inserted, but this was almost an anachronistic feature for the 1960's.

One of Michelotti's brilliant features was this 'Surrey-top' feature. When the TR4 was ordered with a hardtop this came in two pieces — a light-alloy casting which doubled as a roll-hoop and a rear-window support, and a metal roof panel which bolted between the casting and the top of the screen. In place of the roof panel, however, a light frame and a 'hood' panel could be supplied. On the left: the frame. On the right: the 'Surrey-top' in place.

TR4s in production at Coventry. The vast majority are left-hand drive, mainly for export to the United States, and those wooden 'bumpers' are shipping boards for use while the cars are packed close together on the high seas.

38

conditions (and — equally important — in driving tests or low-speed rallying manoeuvres).

As the car had been put into production very rapidly (release of capital investment was delayed in the winter of 1960-61 due to the Standard-Triumph company's financial problems), some changes already intended for the new car were not ready. Starting from Commission Number CT4388 (disc wheels) and CT4690 (wire wheels) — that is to say quite early in 1962 — a new front suspension geometry was introduced, which is recognized by the smooth shape of the top wishbone pressing. Up until then the TR3A wishbone links and geometry had been carried forward unchanged.

At the same time the definitive TR4 braking system was introduced, which meant that the smaller and lighter Girling 16P calliper was fitted, though the rear brakes were not altered. The front brake pad size, too, was reduced, though there is no evidence to suggest that braking performance was in any way impaired; this system, incidentally, would be used on later and much faster TRs without drama.

The next important development changes came along in the winter of 1962-63, though they did not coincide. On and after TR4 body 15076CT (it is not possible to quote an exact Commission Number changeover point due to the way bodies were processed at Canley) the original TR3A seats were supplanted by the definitive TR4 seats, which are easily identified by having much flatter cushions and squabs and an entirely new frame and structure. These basic frames, incidentally, would be used in all subsequent TRs until the onset of United States legislation made yet another design necessary.

The other major innovation was that Zenith-Stromberg Type 175CD carburettors replaced the HS6 SUs which had been fitted to all TRs since the autumn of 1955. There was no dramatic engineering reason for this — the change was influenced entirely by motor industry politics. The SU concern, of course, was controlled by BMC, whereas Zenith were independent. The Stromberg's method of operation was identical with that of the SU — both operate on the constant-vacuum principle with a moving piston lifting a needle out of a fixed central jet — and the Stromberg's introduction took place as soon as SU's master patents expired.

With the new carburettors came a new inlet manifold, identifiable by the smoother shape of the air passages between carburettor and cylinder-head faces. The Stromberg had absolutely no effect on power or torque, and factory testers were usually unable to tell from the driving seat which type of instrument was fitted to a particular TR4.

It was more than a coincidence, incidentally, that the fixing flange and the spacing of fixing holes on that flange were the same on both makes of carburettor. This meant that each could be fitted to either manifold and that conversions were easily arranged.

Perhaps Triumph had this in mind at one stage, and certainly there was a trial production of Stromberg-equipped engines in the winter of 1962-63 before the complete switch was made in the summer of 1963. For the record, the first 100 Stromberg-carburettor TR4 engines were on engines CT16801 to CT16900, and the regular fitments began at CT23594.

In the main, the TR4 had a very placid and successful life. In retrospect it is seen as an interim model, as a replacement was already well into the design stage by the end of 1962, with the first prototype on the road during 1963. Production of the TR4 eventually ceased at the beginning of 1965, after more than 40,000 examples had been made. This figure, in cars per year, approached the heights of TR3A achievement, and proved that Triumph's decision to go for a much better-equipped sports car had been right.

To replace the TR4, from March 1965, they had designed an even more sophisticated car, the TR4A, which was much more radically re-engineered than its title suggests. Whereas the TR3A had been little more than a retouched TR3, the TR4A was altogether different. This author (employed by Triumph at the time) could never understand why it was not named a TR5 right from the start; the official reason was that the TR4 had established itself as a new breed of sports car, and the new model had to be seen as a development of it.

Externally there was little to distinguish a TR4A from a TR4 — it is only a matter of a new front grille, new side flashing indicators and touches of decoration here and there — but there is usually a giveaway in the attitude of the rear wheels. For the kernel of the TR4A's engineering was the new chassis, which included independent rear suspension. This, though not a world first like the TR3's disc brakes, was nevertheless a great advance

The TR4 engine — indistinguishable between 1,991cc and 2,138cc form — installed in the roomy engine bay. The hinge-forward bonnet arrangements are clear in this detail. The recess in the right-side wheel arch is to allow the easy fitment of an optional vacuum brake servo.

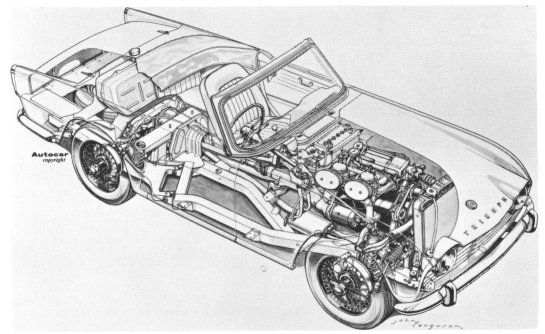

1965 and the next dramatic updating of the TR theme — an entirely new all-independent chassis frame for the TR4A. This Autocar cutaway drawing, which has not been seen before, shows how a much stronger frame had been allied to the TR4 body-shell.

On the left is the TR4 chassis, little modified from 1953 and TR2 days. Compare it with the TR4A chassis layout, which in plan strongly resembled a bell. The independent rear suspension was supported by massively strong box-section members, and to meet increasingly severe noise limitations a more ambitious exhaust system had to be fitted, with twin outlet pipes.

The new independent rear suspension would be shared by all TR4As, TR5s and TR6s except TR4As sold to the United States. Cast semi-trailing arms were pivoted from the chassis frame, the differential casing was hung from the chassis frame, there were coil springs, and the suspension was controlled by lever-arm dampers mounted transversely. Above right: For the United States, where the importers were not willing to impose the cost penalties of independent rear suspension on their TR4A customers, this hybrid solid-rear-axle scheme was built. The chassis frame was basically the same as for the independent TR4As, but without the massive spring bridge-piece.

During the TR4's run the front suspension geometry was revised and the roll-centre raised. At the same time new pressed top wishbones were specified, and the entire assembly was carried forward to the TR4A.

Under-bonnet view of the TR4A, showing the Stromberg 175CD carburettors which had first been used on later-model TR4s and the more efficiently gas-flowed inlet manifolds used with the new carbs. Note that the TR4A's radiator did not have a filler cap extension.

for sports cars of this class, and suddenly made cars like the MGB and the Austin-Healey 3000 look archaic.

An all-independent suspension system, after all, was nothing new to Triumph. Their Heralds had pioneered this in 1959 (even if their system was crude) and the same layout had later been adapted to the Vitesse range and the TR's 'little sister', the Triumph Spitfire. More important, however, was that from the autumn of 1963 Triumph's big saloon, the 2000, had been in production with an all-independent layout. In effect, therefore, the TR4A was merely coming into line with the rest of the Triumph range, and made the marque unique. No other British quantity-production concern was building *all* its cars with independent rear suspension, even in 1965.

The layout of the frame itself was governed by the rear suspension, so this is described first. In general principle and operation, though not in detail, it was like that of the Triumph 2000. Wheel location was by cast-alloy semi-trailing wishbones, suspension was by coil springs mounted ahead of the line of the rear wheels, and the drive-shafts had splines mid-way along their length. Unique to the TR4A were the method of mounting the differential casing to the frame and the fact that lever-arm hydraulic dampers were mounted across the chassis, with short drop-arm links to the semi-trailing wishbones. The Triumph 2000, of course, used long telescopic dampers, for which space could not be found in the TR's package. Nominally, the rear wheels ran with half a degree of positive camber, but there was a tolerance of plus-or-minus one degree on that figure.

The frame, which was always intended to be even stiffer and more sturdy than that of the classic live-axle TRs, had to pick up the splayed pivot axes of the semi-trailing wishbones, the mountings for the differential, and provide support for the rear coil springs and for the newly-positioned dampers. By definition, therefore, it would be a completely different shape from the well-known live-axle frame. As eventually put into production it resembled a bell in plan, and was distinguished by the stout bridge-piece across the rear suspension area.

Elements of the TR4's front suspension were used, but the geometry was revised, with pivot positions 'in space' modified, so that the instantaneous roll-centre was 7.8in off the ground instead of 0.75in, as it had been for the TR4. The TR4's brakes, and the usual choice of disc or wire-spoke wheels, was continued.

Although radial-ply tyres were still not standard, there was an optional choice of covers, including the well-proven Michelin X and the Dunlop SP41.

The complication, however, which is only familiar to United States owners of TR4As, was that provision was made for a live-axle layout, too! This was done to satisfy Triumph's North American importers, who were of the opinion that their customers would not bear the extra cost of irs, would not need it (because of the nature of most roads) and would not appreciate it, either! Therefore, as an option to the independent rear suspension there was also a live-axle TR4A.

This, however, did *not* use the old TR4 chassis, but a specially simplified version of the TR4A design. The pictures make this clear — apart from the presence of the live axle the most obvious difference is the lack of the massive spring/differential chassis bridge-piece. The change was so simply done that the old spring-locating pads on the axle tubes were retained, but unused.

Under the bonnet, there were few changes. The 1,991cc engine option was dropped, and the 2,138cc engine was uprated to 104bhp at 4,700rpm by camshaft profile changes and with a new free-flowing exhaust system. Even so, the TR4A was little faster than before, and the company was beginning to worry about this. In 12 years the outright performance of a TR had barely changed, while most of the competition had progressed in leaps and bounds.

Indeed, in the development stages it had been proposed to make one final and radical change to the TR engine in order to boost performance. In its wet-liner form the engine could not be enlarged much further (TR racing enthusiasts sometimes use performance kits with 87mm liners, but that is the practical limit) so the company proposed to enlarge it by converting the cylinder-block to conventional dry-liner construction. In this way a cylinder bore of 93mm (and a capacity of 2,499cc) could be achieved without making other changes.

However, the problem was that this 'big four' did not release all that much more power than before, even though its torque was substantially improved, and the general refinement of the engine suffered considerably. Therefore, even though this engine was also once mooted for use in the Morgan Plus 4, it was not put into production. Carburation, incidentally, was by twin Zenith-Stromberg units, as had been used on the last run of TR4s, but

The TR4A looked almost identical to the TR4 except for a different radiator grille and the new combined side-lamp housing and decorative wing flash. There was a new bonnet badge, too, but no sheet metal changes.

Triumph boasted only discreetly about their independent rear suspension on the TR4A. It was, after all, a breakthrough for a mass-produced British sports car, only emulated at the time by the more expensive E-Type Jaguar and the TR4A's little sister, the Spitfire.

From the tail, only the badging and the side flash gives a clue that this is a TR4A. The hardtop was optional, as it had been on the TR4, along with the wire wheels.

The TR4A facia was virtually identical with that of the TR4, except that a walnut veneer facia board was standardized. Other features in this view of an export-specification TR4A are the new handbrake location — on top of the tunnel instead of alongside as previously — and the revised seats introduced during the run of the TR4.

An historic, even a sad, moment in the life of the TR sports car. The date is August 2, 1967. Dropping off the line is the very last of the four-cylinder TRs, a TR4A destined for an export customer. Right behind it is the first six-cylinder production TR, a brightly decal-covered TR250 with its 2,498cc engine, which would shortly be shipped to the United States. The reign of the four-banger TR had lasted for 14 years.

from Commission Number CT62191 these were supplanted by SU HS6s — the reverse of the 1963 change!

Other detail changes, all definite improvements, were the specification of a diaphragm-spring clutch for the first time, the fitting of the handbrake on top of the gearbox tunnel (at last that leg-rubbing location alongside the tunnel had gone), and the final deletion of the rather spurious occasional-seat option. An alternator became optional on the engine, and a 'no-loss' system of radiator cooling was standardized.

Even without looking underneath the car it is possible to identify a live-axle TR4A from an all-independent TR4A; those with live-axles are in a CT Commission Number series, whereas those with all-independent suspension are prefixed CTC. The numbering, however, is consecutive. TR enthusiasts will realize that in this case the second 'C' acts as a prefix in the same way as 'L' and 'O' act as suffix identifications for left-hand drive and overdrive, respectively.

The TR4A's life was shorter than that of the TR4; it was on sale for only 30 months, but in that time more than 28,000 cars were made. Somehow, though, impetus was being lost. In spite of the up-to-date chassis and suspension of the TR4A, the car was not as popular as the TR4, and not nearly as successful as the TR3A. It was no longer being considered in the same way as a performance car — the maximum speed was stuck stubbornly at under 110mph, and the factory had stopped using TRs in works competition after 1963.

In 1967, therefore, the factory determined to do something startling about this — and the TR5 was the result.

CHAPTER 4

TRs in competition

Racing and rallying, including the Twin-Cams

Before the development of the Triumph TR2, Standard-Triumph had no competitions department and took no interest in motor sport. Two things helped to change this situation — Ken Richardson was very keen on racing and rallying, and it was also immediately obvious that people were ordering TR2s in 1953 and 1954 with the definite intention of using them in all types of motor sport. A department would have to be set up to provide advice and to develop special parts.

The factory therefore established a competitions department in 1954, and this has been active, with some gaps, ever since. There have been three distinct phases, as follows:

1954-1961 Department managed by Ken Richardson, racing and rallying TR2, TR3 and TR3A models, plus racing the special twin-cam TR3S and TRS Le Mans cars. Based at Banner Lane (housed in the experimental department), Allesley (in the service department) and finally at Radford.

1962-1967 Department managed by Graham Robson, rallying TR4s until 1964. Later managed by Ray Henderson running other models. At Fletchamstead North, next to the experimental department.

1969 to date Department managed successively by Peter Browning, Basil Wales and Bill Price, running various Triumph models. TR7s rallied since 1976. Based at the MG factory at Abingdon, in the British Leyland competitions centre.

Although the most interesting of all these cars were the Le Mans twin-cams, historically they developed from normal production TR3s, and I must describe these cars first. In 1954

and 1955, in any case, Ken Richardson's department ran TR2s in major rallies *and* races, and at least one works machine competed in both types of event.

Assembling a complete list of activities for the Richardson era has been very difficult as all the department's written records were apparently destroyed when it was closed down in 1961. However, careful research through company and sporting magazine files has revealed what I think is a comprehensive list of the cars and their uses. I must mention, however, that 'semi-works' cars existed then, as they do today, just to confuse the matter!

The TR's first successes, in 1954, were achieved by private owners. The fact that many early (1953-54) TR2s were registered in Coventry before delivery is confusing, as these cars were not connected with the works team. The TR2 which took 15th place at Le Mans in 1954 was registered OKV 777, but crewed by Wadsworth and Dickson (and owned by Dickson's Triumph dealership). Johnny Wallwork's own TR2 which won the 1954 RAC Rally was, however, registered in his native Stockport.

The factory team almost always used up-to-the-minute models, and soon sold off those made obsolete by technical changes in production cars. Thus TR2s were used in 1954-55, TR3s in 1956 (and with disc brakes in 1957), and TR3As (sometimes with 2.2-litre engines) from 1958 to 1960. TR4s were used from 1962 to 1964 (in 2-litre and 2.2-litre form), while 16-valve 2-litre TR7s have been campaigned in 1976 and 1977.

Over the years there have been three distinct attitudes to tuning and modification. In the Richardson era, no serious attempt was ever made to improve the cars by power tuning or by making

The combination of Maurice Gatsonides and a TR sports car notched up many successes in international rallying in the 1950's. PDU 20 was one of the three original 1954 team cars, and was co-driven by Rob Slotemaker in the Alpine Rally that year.

The first official works competition TR2 — OVC 276 — in its Mille Miglia race trim and with Ken Richardson at the wheel. In the race he shared the driving with Maurice Gatsonides. Note that although this was a British-registered TR2 it had left-hand drive.

One privately-owned TR2 (OKV 777) had raced at Le Mans in 1954 in standard trim, but the factory entered three special TR2s for the 1955 race. The cars were PKV 374/375/376, and each was equipped with a different set of prototype disc brakes for proving and test purposes. All three cars finished, the fastest of them being PKV 376, driven by Bobbie Dickson and Ninian Sanderson, which averaged 84.4mph and took 14th place. Apart from the disc brakes and obvious race fittings the cars were virtually standard.

Leslie Brooke pulling away from a pit stop in the 1955 Le Mans race in one of the works TR2s.

This is a familiar picture of the five TR3s which all took *Coupes* for unpenalized runs in the 1956 Alpine Rally. The three nearest the camera — SRW 992, SRW 991, and SRW 410 — are works team cars, driven respectively by Tommy Wisdom, Paddy Hopkirk and Maurice Gatsonides. All three ran as Grand Touring cars; the exterior door handles which were part of the 'kit' can be seen on Wisdom's car. The front tyres on that car, incidentally, are completely bald. The other private cars were driven by the Kat brothers (SXK 4) and by Leslie Griffiths (VYD 797).

Paddy Hopkirk's TR3 nearing the top of the Stelvio on the 1956 Alpine Rally. In that year his car survived impeccably and helped him to an unpenalized run; two years later he was not so lucky.

The factory ran TR3s with front disc brakes for just one season — 1957 — after which they were replaced by TR3As. Above left is Bernard Consten's car on its way to third overall on the incredibly tough Liège-Rome-Liège. The other two cars finished fifth and ninth, and won the coveted Manufacturer's Team Prize. Above is a 1958 Alpine Rally shot proving that even a hard-sprung TR3A team car could be persuaded to take up an attitude of roll! This was one of the quintet of apple-green cars used throughout 1958, and is being driven towards a second place in class by Ian Titterington. This was the event when Triumph surprised everyone by turning up with an 86mm-bore 2,138cc engine and defeating all the bigger Austin-Healeys.

The final set of team TR3As were the 'WVC' cars — 247/248/249/250 — used during 1959 and 1960. Here is a mud-spattered but healthy WVC at the finish of the 1960 Tulip Rally, driven by Rob Slotemaker and Ron Crellin, and beaten, incidentally, by David Seigle-Morris' privately-prepared TR3A!

them lighter. When TR4s were used these were progressively tuned, modified and lightened as far as the regulations (and budgets!) would allow. Now, with the more recent TR7s, building them to the Appendix J Group 4 limits has allowed such features as rear-wheel disc brakes, 16-valve engines (when only the eight-valve engine was on general sale), and twin double-choke Weber carburettors to be specified.

Although the Richardson cars were usually reliable and always well-prepared, they were no faster than standard. Therefore, privately-owned cars could be and sometimes were faster than the team cars, and towards the end of the TR3A's use this trend was becoming a little embarrassing. The only important specification changes made between 1954 and 1960 were to axle ratios, to the hardtop bodywork (where a simple and effective kit allowed the TRs to be classed as Grand Tourers if the regulations for an event were favourable) and to the *size* of the engine.

The 86mm bore, 2,138cc engine was developed initially for Richardson's team cars to use — where the class in which they competed had an upper limit of 2,500cc — and was a simple conversion, but no power tuning modifications were applied to it. From 1958 onwards, a team car would be entered with either of the engines, depending on the appropriate class limits.

The light-blue TR4s used from 1962 to 1964 — there were only ever four of them, with consecutive registrations, and only one now remains in Great Britain — were progressively developed. In their first event they were mechanically almost standard, but later they had complete light-alloy body skin panels and doors, limited-slip differentials, and engines having twin double-choke Weber carburettors and tubular exhaust manifolds.

In modern times, the Group 4 TR7s are not allowed to use lightweight panels, but engine tuning is substantially free and suspension changes are allowed — which explains why the first four team cars had different rear-axle locations, a choice of transmissions (including overdrive behind the four-speed box, not a known production specification) and very 'hot' 200bhp engines. Development continues.

The first competition success by a TR2 came in January 1954 when a Coventry-registered but privately-owned car driven by Chester motor trader Denis Done won a club rally in North Wales. It was not very significant, but it was a start.

The breakthrough, at International level, came in March 1954 when Johnny Wallwork took his own TR2 to an outright win in the British RAC Rally, defeating the works team of Sunbeam-Talbots and Ian Appleyard's Jaguar XK120 in the process. Neither was it a fluke performance, as Peter Cooper's TR2 was second and Bill Bleakley's TR2 fifth.

The very first works TR2 was OVC 276, driven by Ken Richardson and Maurice Gatsonides in the 1954 Mille Miglia. A flat-out run for 1,000 miles (using, incidentally, 16in wire wheels) among a fleet of Ferraris, Lancias and Maseratis, resulted in 27th overall at an average of 73mph. Edgar Wadsworth and Bobbie Dickson then showed that a private car could also race with the élite by averaging 74.7mph in atrocious weather in the Le Mans 24-hours race and finishing 15th.

To round off a very fine start to its racing career, the TR2 then figured strongly in the Tourist Trophy race at Dundrod, where six cars started (one of them Dickson's ex-Le Mans OKV 777) and all six finished, to take the team prize in a most convincing manner.

The rallying team, too, started with a flourish. Three team cars tackled the fast and gruelling French Alpine Rally in mid-summer, where Gatsonides and Rob Slotemaker won a *Coupe des Alpes* for an unpenalized run, and the factory lifted the team prize at their very first attempt.

The next season was dislocated by the Le Mans tragedy and its effect on the entire sporting scene. Carnage caused when Levegh's 300SLR Mercedes-Benz ploughed into the grandstand overshadowed the fact that three experimental TR2s, all with experimental disc-brake systems, were entered by the Triumph factory and all finished strongly. The running average of 84.4mph was much higher than that of Wadsworth's 1954 entry, but due to more reliable running and drier weather rather than increased performance. One car had four-wheel Dunlop discs (with servo), and the others had Girling front discs and drum rears, without servo.

The team had no success in the Tulip Rally (where handicaps often made sure that a sports car would be struggling) but in the gruelling Liège-Rome-Liège the redoubtable Richardson took fifth overall and established the TR tradition on that event.

By 1956 the TR3 was recognized as *the* car for a private owner to buy as it was so versatile. In that year the factory dominated the results in the French Alpine Rally, and TR3s won no fewer than

An excuse to use this picture is that the author is co-driving John Sprinzel in the 1962 Tulip Rally in one of the four powder-blue TR4s used by the reformed competitions department. This car subsequently went to Canada for the 1964 Shell 4000 Rally, rebuilt and reregistered . . .

. . . as did 5VC, Jean-Jacques Thuner's regular car, which was driven by him along with Roy Fidler. In final form the 2.2-litre engines with Weber carburettors produced about 130bhp, and the cars had light-alloy skin panels.

Downfall of the TR4s was the rough roads used in rallies of the 1960's. This is Roy Fidler in 6VC, once the spare car, but regularly pressed into service. The front wing vents are to allow hot air to escape from the under-bonnet area. Bumpers have been removed because the regulations allowed it. On these cars there was a fixed cold-air scoop ahead of the windscreen instead of the flap fitted to production cars.

4VC is the most noted of all TR4 team cars, for Mike Sutcliffe and Roy Fidler drove it to a splendid fourth overall in the 1962 Alpine Rally (and a *Coupe*), beaten only by two 3-litre Austin-Healeys and a very special Porsche Carrera. This is the only team TR4 which remains in Great Britain.

At a casual glance this could be a race-prepared TR3, but closer examination reveals that it is one of the three (XHP 938/939/940) TR3S Le Mans cars of 1959. Though superficially like the TR3A in shape the cars had a longer wheelbase, glass-fibre body-shells, and of the course the now-famous 'Sabrina' twin-cam 2-litre engine. In TR3S guise the cars had normal-type TR3 tracks.

This side view of the TR3S 1959 Le Mans car clearly shows the increased wheelbase. The six inches (an increase duplicated in the 'Zoom' project — see Chapter 7) was inserted between the front wheels and the doors. The profile of the front wings is an important bit different from a normal TR3A. The car had all-round disc brakes, but a remarkably standard specification apart from the engine.

Above: Under-side view of a TR3S showing the more robust chassis (with increased-depth side-members) but the broadly similar layout to the production cars. The axle, however, is stronger than the TR3A item and is specially cooled, and the front suspension has an anti-roll bar. Above right: Officially known as the TRS twin-cam engine, but unofficially as 'Sabrina', the Le Mans 2-litre unit was always raced with two twin-choke SU carburettors, and gave between 150 and 160bhp. The five-layer 'sandwich' method of construction is clear in this view, as are the front timing-wheel covers which gave rise to the very apt nickname. The engine's bore and stroke were 90mm and 78mm, respectively. One engine — in the 1961 Conrero-Triumph — had twin double-choke Webers, and a road version had twin single-choke SUs and milder camshaft profiles.

The rear-wheel disc brakes, the sturdier chassis frame and the bigger dampers complete with adjustable settings are all obvious in this TR3S detail shot.

five *Coupes* and collected the team prize as if it were their right.

The TR success story now begins to get a little boring, if only because it was so predictable. Although a TR never again won a major race or rally outright (the team cars were always too standard for that) class wins were usually there for the asking and team prizes, too, if enough of the cars were entered.

Their versatility was astonishing. In 1957, for example, Bernard Consten took third place in the Liège-Rome-Liège, by now recognized as the toughest of all events, while a trio of updated 1956 rally cars were sent to the Sebring 12-hours race to take an untroubled class win.

Next year, 1958, was noted for several things. Triumph introduced the TR3A rally cars, painted in a fetching and rare apple-green, had a new lady driver, Annie Soisbault, who so nearly won the European Ladies' Rally Championship, and used the 86mm bore, 2,138cc engine for the first time. In the Alpine Rally the 2.2-litre engine was used to such effect that the TRs defeated the entire team of 2.6-litre Austin-Healeys. Gatsonides also achieved fifth overall in the Liège-Rome-Liège in the same Alpine class-winning machine.

By 1959, with more attention focussed on the twin-cam Le Mans cars, development of the rally team tended to stagnate. However, with a brand-new set of bright-red TR3As the team tackled many events, and Annie Soisbault made another very determined attack on the Ladies' Championship (at the end of the season she tied with an expensively-sponsored girl in a Volvo). Four class wins — in Holland, Greece, France and Belgium — with team prizes in the German and RAC Rallies, were typical of the team's fortunes.

The same cars were kept on for 1960, when the most important result was the defeat of the works team in the Tulip Rally by private-owner David Seigle-Morris in his own TR3A. David was signed-on for the Alpine to drive a team car, when he beat them all again! That was the final flourish for the rallying team, which was then disbanded in favour of Le Mans racing.

With the increasingly-special TR4s used in Europe in 1962 and 1963, the problem was that events were becoming rougher and yet rougher. A TR4 was really no match for conditions in the forests (the RAC Rally), nor for the boulders (Yugoslavia and Bulgaria on the Liège), so it could only shine on tarmac, in the Tulip and the Alpine. Mike Sutcliffe's fourth overall, with a

Coupe des Alpes, in the 1962 Alpine was a case in point, but in 1963 even the brilliant driving of Vic Elford (third fastest on scratch in the Tulip behind a 3-litre Austin-Healey and a 4·7-litre Ford Falcon) couldn't beat the handicaps which European rallying provided.

The team won prizes in the 1962 RAC Rally, the 1963 Tulip Rally and — in re-registered form — in the 1964 Shell 4000 Rally in Canada, but not even the lightest possible bodies and the most powerful engines could make them competitive any more. For 1964 they were replaced by the big Triumph 2000 saloons for the rough, and by the jewel-like Spitfire competition cars for Le Mans and the tarmac rallies.

Most recently, TR7s have been used by British Leyland as the spearhead of the Group's entire rallying programme. So far they have suffered a lack of razor-edge engine development (it is now necessary to have at least 120bhp per litre — which would mean 240bhp from the 16-valve Dolomite Sprint-type engine — to be competitive), but the cars have already proved very strong and they handle well. At the time of writing the Abingdon team have only prepared four cars — KDU 497N and KDU 498N, along with OOE 937R and OOE 938R — and their most spectacular win has been by Tony Pond in the Boucles de Spa, early in 1977. Pond was also in the money on the 1977 Scottish (second) and the 1977 Mintex (third). The team's best results still lie ahead; as their car experience builds up and engines are further developed they will become increasingly more competitive. By the time this book is published I am sure Abingdon will have notched up more wins.

Apart from the TR7s, quite a number of the ex-works team cars are now in private hands, but most unfortunately not in their original condition. The three blue TR4s which contested the 1964 Shell 4000 Rally were sold in North America, as were the 1957 Sebring cars.

Competition items developed by the Ken Richardson department and suitable for fitment to TR2, TR3, TR3A and often TR4 models, were catalogued for years. These items are confined to things like sump shields, oil-cooler kits, anti-roll bars and the like. No engine tune-up kits were ever offered, though TR4 items included officially-approved SAH parts (manifolds and camshaft).

Separate from all this production-car activity was the saga of the

In 1960 a quartet of new Le Mans cars, the TRSs, were built, and these raced at Le Mans in 1960 and 1961. The chassis and mechanicals were basically as for the TR3S, except that the wide wheel tracks of the 'Zoom/Zest' project were used, along with rack-and-pinion steering. The new glass-fibre bodies were shaped like those of the long-wheelbase 'Zooms', and the cars were registered 926/927/928/929 HP.

Pre-race modifications in 1960 included stoneguards behind the rear wheels and a matt finish for the previously chrome-plated windscreen supports and giant filler cap.

Three detail TRS shots. Above left: This was the under-bonnet view (with twin-circuit brakes seen clearly). Left: The cockpit and facia, awaiting the arrival of the windscreen. Above: The boot, with the big petrol tank exposed. The toolkit (right) and the bottle jack (left) were a wise precaution in case of on-circuit dramas.

None of the TR3S cars finished at Le Mans in 1959 — two due to the trivial failure of fan blades, which then punctured the water radiators. This is the Jopp/Stoop machine (Dickie Stoop driving) which retired after 22 hours when lying seventh overall and leading its class. Its best lap speed was 105mph.

The Le Mans line-up for 1960, with overalled engine-king Ted Silver easing back 928HP to get it into position.

1961, and the same four TRS cars roll off the transporter before the Le Mans race. A comparison with the previous picture shows that 929HP was the unused car in 1960, while 928HP stood idle in 1961. The 1960 cars had no wing air vents, but these were added in time for the 1961 race.

Les Leston in the 1960 TRS at Le Mans.

Le Mans cars, with their very special twin-cam engines. The engine was designed first (primarily as a competition 2-litre unit, but with a definite eye to detuning for road use in projected TR4s), and the cars which first used it were built in 1958 and first raced in 1959. There were two distinct breeds, one descending from the other, and the evolution needs careful explanation.

In 1959, the original Le Mans cars looked like race-prepared TR3As, and were known as TR3S models. However they had a wheelbase six inches longer than standard (the extra space was inserted between the front suspension and the toe-board) and had glass-fibre bodies. The chassis and suspension were substantially standard, except that the main side members were deeper and therefore stronger, the back axles were stronger and of a non-standard type, and Girling disc brakes were fitted all round. There were three of these machines — XHP 938, XHP 939 and XHP 940 — all of which raced at Le Mans. The engines were built-up from a series of sandwich-type light-alloy castings, with a five-bearing crankshaft and topped by a twin-overhead-camshaft cylinder-head having very prominent covers over the timing wheels at the front. Inevitably (because of the popularity of a well-endowed show-girl of the period) the engine was nicknamed Sabrina! Two twin-choke SU carburettors were standard, and more than 150bhp was produced. Unfortunately, all three retired from the race, two when their fan blades flew off and wrecked the cooling radiators, and the last with an oil pump failure when leading its class.

A year later a quartet of TRS cars appeared. These, while philosophically similar to the TR3S, were much different in detail. The original three cars had been scrapped and their mechanical components were revamped for 1960. The new chassis differed in that they had increased wheel tracks and rack-and-pinion steering (as already intended for the TR4), while the new-shape glass-fibre bodies were identical with those of the 'Zoom' prototypes being developed by the factory as a TR3A replacement (see Chapter 7).

In 1960 the engines were almost the same as in 1959, but ran without fans. All three cars finished the Le Mans race, and the fastest lapped at 102mph, but valve stretch caused a loss of power and none completed the minimum distance necessary to qualify.

In 1961 the factory's policy was dramatically vindicated. Three TRSs started, three finished, and they won the much-coveted Le Mans team prize. The fastest of all finished ninth overall and averaged 98.9mph, the others averaging 97.2 and 91.2mph, respectively. Keith Ballisat and Peter Bolton were the drivers of the best-placed TRS, and apart from having slightly uprated engines the Triumphs were almost identical with the 1960 cars. The fastest race lap went up to 105mph. The TRS cars carried the registration numbers 926 HP, 927 HP, 928 HP and 929 HP — 929 HP did not race in 1960, and 928 HP stood down in 1961. These cars were subequently sold off in the United States, where some at least have been restored and are seen at Vintage Triumph Register meetings.

There was one other competition prototype — the 'Conrero' TRS Le Mans car — built in 1960-61, but this was not completed before the Richardson department was closed down, and was also subsequently sold off to North America, where it lives on. Registered 3097 VC, with chassis number X707, the Conrero-Triumph had a much-modified chassis, and a closed two-seater coupe body-shell shaped by Michelotti. Under the bonnet was the very rare twin-Weber-carburettor version of the Sabrina engine.

Apart from the fact that a suitably prepared TR2 or early TR3 was a very strong contender for fuel economy contests, there was no doubt that the cars' rugged reliability made record attempts attractive, too. In July 1959 a team of Cambridge University undergraduates used XHP 259, as prepared by the factory, to break eight International Class E records at up to 102mph and up to 10,000 kilometres; not bad for a £900 sports car!

Private owners, of course, and dealer-sponsored cars all over the world won hundreds, perhaps thousands, of events in their own TRs. It might be a Macau Grand Prix, or a navigational rally in the USA. It might be a British night rally, or one of the 'home' Internationals, a club race, or a long-distance sports car race — there would usually be at least one TR in the entry list. If only the factory had pursued a more aggressive attitude to special competition fittings (as did their rivals, BMC) then the list of wins by cars in the TR range might have been even longer.

The Becquart/Rothschild TRS making a pit stop in the 1961 Le Mans race. Ken Richardson is bendıng down to peer under the car, Ray Henderson (in cap) is closing the bonnet, while Les Makinson (experimental department foreman) looks after refuelling.

65

An infamous occasion, which caused Paddy Hopkirk to be sacked from the works team and brought the retirement of a factory TR3A. VRW 220, climbing the Stelvio pass in the 1958 Alpine Rally, complete with flailing punctured rear tyre. The effort cooked the 2.2-litre engine and Hopkirk's rally was over.

Future World Champion racing driver Phil Hill raced a TR2 in the United States in the 1950's; it was a 'long door' 1954 model.

PHIL HILL, noted Sports Car Driver, seated in the Triumph TR-2 Competition Car.

Bob Tullius used a TR4 to great effect in SCCA races of the early 1960s . . .

. . . and later went even faster in an enormously rapid TR6.

A rally Triumph TR7, crewed by Tony Pond/Fred Gallagher, beats a path to a second overall finish on the very rough Lombard-Esso Scottish Rally (June 4-7, 1977). Leyland's team of two TR7s and a Triumph Dolomite Sprint won the Manufacturers' Team Award on this major international event.

The 16-valve TR7 engine compartment — 1977 rally car specification. The brace links the strut tops to give added rough-road rigidity. The complex extra electric circuitry and the pipework to the oil cooler are all visible.

Works competition cars used by Triumph since 1954

1954	TR2	OVC 276	PDU 20	PDU 21	For racing and rallying
1955	TR2	OVC 276	PDU 21	PKV 693	
		PKV 697	PKV 698	RHP 557	
		PKV 374	PKV 375	PKV 376	These three were Le Mans cars
1956	TR3	SHP 520	SRW 410	SRW 991	
		SRW 992			
1957	TR3	SRW 410	SRW 991	SRW 992	Raced at Sebring
		SHP 520			Raced in Mille Miglia
		SKV 656	TRW 735	TRW 736	
		TRW 737			
1958	TR3A	VRW 219	VRW 220	VRW 221	
		VRW 223	VHP 529	VWK 610	
		WDU 712	VVC 672	VVC 673	
1959	TR3A	WVC 247	WVC 248	WVC 249	
		WVC 250	XHP 259		
	TR3S	XHP 938	XHP 939	XHP 940	Le Mans twin-cams, TR3A shape
1960	TR3A	WVC 247	WVC 248	WVC 249	
		WVC 250	XHP 259		
	TRS	926 HP	927 HP	928 HP	Le Mans twin-cams, 'Zoom' shape
		929 HP			

1961	TRS	926 HP	927 HP	928 HP	
		929 HP			
1962	TR4	3 VC	4 VC	5 VC	Light-alloy-skinned coupes
		6 VC			
1963	TR4	3 VC	4 VC	5 VC	
		6 VC			
1964	TR4	3 VC	5 VC	6 VC	All given United States registrations for Shell 4000 Rally
1976	TR7	KDU 497N	KDU 498N	OOE 937R	
		OOE 938R			
1977	TR7	KDU 497N	KDU 498N	OOE 937R	
		OOE 938R	OOM 512R	OOM 513R	
		OOM 514R	SCE 645S ★		
1978	TR7	OOM 513R	SJW 533S		
	TR7V8	KDU 497N	OOM 512R	SJW 533S	
		SJW 540S	SJW 548S		
1979	TR7V8	OOM 514R	SJW 533S	SJW 540S	
		SJW 546S	SJW 548S	UYH 863S	
		TUD 682T	TUD 683T	XJO 414V	
1980	TR7V8	SJW 546S	UYH 863S	TUD 683T	
		TUD 686T	XJO 414V	HRW 250V	
		HRW 251V	JJO 931W		

★ *Built for Abingdon by Safety Devices, Cambridge, for the 1977 RAC Rally*

CHAPTER 5

Six-cylinder TRs — 1967 to 1976

TR5, TR250 and TR6

Wednesday, August 2, 1967, was a sad day for the 'classic' TR enthusiast. On that day, as an illustration in this book shows, the very last of the TR4As was built in Coventry. When the TR5s and TR250s which replaced the TR4A were publicly announced in October 1967 they cut off the last mechanical links with the TR's notable past. Although the traditions would continue, a new pedigree was being born.

Until then, every TR sold had been powered by the legendary wet-liner four-cylinder engine, a development of that originally designed in 1945-46 for the Standard Vanguard. Now the TRs would be built with an entirely different dry-liner six-cylinder unit.

The original TR pedigree had been discarded in three stages between 1961 and 1967 — body style first, chassis later, and engine last of all. The TR5 was the model which signalled the end of Triumph's interim period. The TR4 had effectively been a classic TR with a new body, while the TR4A had been given a new all-independent chassis under that body. Now, with the TR5/TR250, a different engine had — at last — arrived.

The use of a six-cylinder engine was not a new idea at all. Ever since the late-1950's there had been experimental TRs running around with six-cylinder engines, but for many years the sales organization had shied away from the very idea; somehow they could not see a TR as a smooth and refined car. It was only the urgent need for more TR performance in the mid-1960's which caused their change of heart.

As already noted in the previous chapter, it was becoming clear that a considerable power boost was needed for future TRs, or the model would surely slip out of the best-selling charts. At least

Triumph's management were astute enough to realise this — unlike MG, who have been stuck with the same MGB for 15 years, and a performance which is now almost embarrassingly slow for marketing needs. Throughout the 1960's every successive model of Austin-Healey 3000 had gone faster, and motor industry gossip indicated that a six-cylinder MGB might also be on the way.

There was no rigid reason why a 'new' TR (which incidentally was called TR4B internally for some time) should have a different engine. However, as there was no practical way in which the old four-cylinder unit's power could be boosted, an alternative had to be found.

There were two possible units in existence at Standard-Triumph when work began in 1965 — a six-cylinder engine and a brand-new vee-8. The vee-8 was such a new design (it was intended for the Stag and possibly for an up-market version of the Triumph 2000 saloon) that it was not to run even in experimental form until 1966, and as it was also potentially so much more expensive, it had to be discarded. At that time, however, it was a 2½-litre unit, and *mechanically* it would have been ideal for the purpose.

This left the existing Triumph 2000 six-cylinder engine, which in its present state of tune was not at all promising. Although it was almost exactly the same capacity — 1,998cc instead of 1,991cc or 2,138cc for the 'four' — it was neither powerful enough nor torquey enough. Fortunately for our story, however, work was in hand to rectify these shortcomings.

The engine itself had interesting design antecedents, which go right back to the end of the 1940's. By then Standard-Triumph

First of a new breed — the six-cylinder TRs — was the TR5, announced in the autumn of 1967, and destined for only a 15-month production run. Once again there were no sheet-metal changes from the TR4A, or even the TR4. The decorative side flashes were retained, but there was a new bonnet badge. The disc-wheel car (see the TR250 illustration) had dummy 'Rostyle' wheel-trims, complete even to dummy wheel nuts. Wire wheels, as ever, were optional. The exterior mirror was standard. All TR5s had the newly-developed 2,498cc six-cylinder engine with fuel injection, giving no less than 150bhp. The bonnet bulge was now superfluous, but would not be eliminated until the shell was restyled for the TR6.

Three-quarter rear view of the new TR5 pinpoints the new badging, the paired exhaust outlets under the far bumper over-rider and the '2500' badge on each rear wing, with indicator repeaters underneath them. The 'PI', of course, stands for Petrol Injection.

For the North American market only, the TR250 took the place of the TR5, which was never sold there. Apart from the special colour schemes, which included transverse speed stripes across the nose of the car, and the badging, all TR250s had a detuned 2,498cc engine with twin carburettors in order to meet the United States anti-emission laws which had come into force. Those wheel trims, even the wheel nuts, are false; when removed, a normal TR4A disc wheel is revealed.

The America-only TR250 with its distinctive badges.

engineers had produced, in double-quick time, the Triumph 1800 Saloon and Roadster, the Standard Vanguard and the Triumph Mayflower. Even before they settled down to tackle the design of the TR2 the Vanguard had been re-bodied, and work had begun on a completely new small car.

This little saloon, the Standard Eight, was new from end to end, and featured a simple but efficient little long-stroke overhead-valve four-cylinder engine. For the record, this unit was of 803cc, with a bore and stroke of 58mm by 76mm, and produced 26bhp at 4,500rpm. Not, at that stage, an engine of interest to TR fans!

Two factors, however, changed all this. One was that the need for more small-car performance over the years had led the engine designers to discover that considerable 'stretch' had been built in to the unit (they had certainly not built it in to the design intentionally!), and the other was that the directors had decided they needed a new engine to replace the wet-liner Vanguard unit at the end of the 1950's.

Fortunately, the machine tooling and the transfer-line installations were adaptable to four-cylinder or six-cylinder blocks, and consequently a straight-six — effectively a 'four' with two extra cylinders tacked on to the end — could be made in a straight-forward fashion.

Stretching the engine went like this:

803cc to 948cc 'four' by a bore increase from 58mm to 63mm.
948cc to 1,147cc 'four' by a further bore increase from 63mm to 69.3mm.
Introduction of 1,998cc 'six' with a new bore dimension of 74.7mm.

That was in 1960, and later things got even more complicated as the little 'four' was stretched, again first to 1,296cc and finally to 1,493cc, and the 'six' was reduced to 1,596cc with a 66.7mm bore for the Vitesse sports-saloon.

The 1,998cc six-cylinder unit was used in the Vanguard Six until 1963, and thereafter in tuned form in the Triumph 2000. By 1965, too, it had been tried in the 'Fury' sports-car project (see Chapter 7) and was earmarked for use in the little GT6 coupe.

Even though the engines had been super-tuned for use in the factory's Triumph 2000 rally cars there was still a problem. With triple twin-choke Weber carburettors and a wild camshaft profile the 1,998cc units could produce 150bhp (gross), but the fuel consumption was horrifying, the flexibility negligible and the cost daunting. As that sort of power was needed for a new TR (but it had to be flexible and refined power) there was a problem.

Once again, two solutions were found, one directly caused by the onset of North American anti-emission regulations. Technical chief Harry Webster's solution to finding more torque was to enlarge the engine still further, while attempts to tackle emissions were centred around fuel injection.

There was no more 'stretch' inside the engine for further cylinder bore enlargements, so Triumph took the bold step of increasing the stroke. This was a startling decision, for in the 1960's all the trends were towards *over-square* engines. The 'stroking' solution would put the engine's bore/stroke ratio back by a decade, but it was completed nevertheless. For the first time this engine family was to be built without the 76mm stroke 'trade mark'; henceforth it would be 95mm. This was not achieved by a simple drawing change — the crankshaft was substantially redesigned, as was the cylinder block. At the same time a new cylinder-head was being developed, so there was little commonality between the new '2.5' unit and the original Triumph 2000 engine.

When the TR5 (always coded 'Wasp' by Triumph's engineering department) was being developed, it became clear that there had to be two different engine specifications for the first time on a TR — the 'de-toxed' version for North America and the more powerful version for the rest of the world. In 1966 a season's racing in the British Saloon Car Championship with a Triumph 2000 had shown that the Lucas fuel-injection package could tame a phenomenally 'wild' camshaft much more successfully than the Webers had done on the rally cars, so this was chosen for production use, albeit with a much more sensible camshaft profile. Surprisingly, however, twin Stromberg carburettors were found to do a very adequate job on the 'federal' engines, and had the additional advantage of being very much cheaper!

Development of the engine was the kernel to the new breed of TR, which was otherwise prepared smoothly and at great speed. But not only would there be different engine specifications this time, but different model names, and the time has now come to explain these.

At this point Triumph had decided that if their 'federal' car was to be very different from the others, it might as well *look* rather

Right: TR5 and TR250 facias were the same. This is a TR250 (with left-hand drive). Note the new 'safety' knobs and switches and the TR4A steering wheel, complete with safety padding on the spokes and a padded rim. The 'eye-ball' fresh-air vents were a useful innovation. With each successive model variant TR interiors were becoming more plushy and better equipped. Below: These were the seats first introduced in mid-run for the TR4, then used on the TR4A and later on the TR5s. In this application they are on a TR4A. Below right: The splendid 150bhp 2,498cc six-cylinder engine developed for the new TR5, and later adapted for the 2.5 PI saloon. The vital metering unit is hidden behind the distributor shaft, from which the petrol, metered accurately at high pressure, was fed out through individual plastic pipes to injectors in the inlet manifolds. The alternator was standardized for all TRs from this variant.

74

The fuel-injected six-cylinder engine installed in the TR5. In fact it was squeezed in with very little trouble, though the radiator had to be pushed forward a little from the TR4A position. The vacuum servo is direct-acting, and changes sides with the pedals. The air cleaner is mounted in front of the radiator, and clean air is fed to the engine through a flexible tube.

The TR250 had this version of the six-cylinder engine, with twin horizontal Stromberg 175CD carburettors. This car always had left-hand drive, as shown by the brake servo, which is nearest the camera in this illustration.

To accommodate the longer six-cylinder engine for the TR5/TR250 the TR4A chassis needed minor modifications. There were new pressings in the region of the front-suspension towers and the bracing cross-tube had to be cranked forward to give clearance for the front of the engine and the plastic fan. Radial-ply tyres (these are Goodyear G800s) were standard.

From January 1969 both the TR5 and the TR250 were replaced by the TR6. Although this retained the basic body engineering of the TR4 shell of 1961, both the nose and the tail areas were substantially restyled by Karmann of Germany. This entailed, in this view, new front wings, a new bonnet (at last without the unnecessary 'power bulge') and a new grille. At first the TR6 had the 'Rostyle' wheels of the TR5/TR250, but the attractive wheels on this car were standardized from the end of 1969.

different, *and* have its own title. Thus was the TR250 born, and since it is much more numerous than the TR5 from which it evolved, it should be described first.

First and foremost, to the relief of the sales organization, Triumph's North American importers decided to drop their demand for an alternative live-axle car. The TR4As of 1965-67, therefore, are the only TRs ever sold with the new chassis but with a live-axle beam. This apart, the TR250 had the same basic chassis as the TR4A and almost the same body. Externally, of course, a TR250 can be identified by its extrovert colour scheme (which includes speed stripes across the bonnet and the front wings) and by the badges. There was a new grille and new decorative details, but otherwise it was much like the TR4A. The chassis frame was only altered slightly to allow the rather longer six-cylinder engine to fit in smoothly. The cross-bracing tube was re-bowed, and there were several detail changes in the pressing work around the nose of the frame.

The brakes now had a servo, fat radial-ply tyres were standard, and the normal TR4A disc wheels were covered with rather horrid 'dummy' Rostyle wheel-trims in which wheel nuts were included. It was unworthy of Triumph, but at least it was a lot cheaper than opting for the real thing! Inside the car the padded steering-wheel spokes and the 'safety' knobs and switches were obvious, and the eye-ball fresh-air vents were a useful innovation.

For the rest of the world (for which rather fewer cars were to be made) the new car would be the TR5. This would have a very powerful (150bhp) 2,498cc engine, compared with the 104bhp of the de-toxed variety. To cope with it, the gearing was raised substantially, and the new 3.45:1 back axle was both new and stronger than anything used before. At a stroke the TR's performance was transformed. Maximum speed was up to around 120mph, and the car could sprint to 100mph in less than half-a-minute whereas a TR4A had struggled to reach the same figure in 50 seconds. Fuel economy, naturally, suffered considerably, but the new owners did not seem to mind.

Incidentally, although the TR5's fuel-injected engine was unique at first, it was already planned for use (in de-tuned form) in the Triumph 2.5PI saloon which followed it a year later, in the autumn of 1968. The carburettor-equipped 2,498cc engine, however, would not be used in another car until the Triumph 2500TC saloon was announced in May 1974. By then, as we shall

see, time was running out for this particular breed of TR.

As it happened, the TR5 and TR250 models had a very short life — only 15 months — because of a snap decision by the directors to go for a speedy restyle of the same basic body. For those who care about these things, therefore, it should be noted that only 2,947 TR5s were built (Commission Number series CP1 to CP3096, with a few gaps), and that there were a total of 8,484 TR250s (CD1 to CD8594). Of the TR5 total, only 1,161 cars stayed in Britain, where they are already something of a collector's item.

Once again, Triumph looked elsewhere for a new body style. Had there been time they would certainly have allowed Michelotti to re-work his original TR4 creation, but the Italian was fully committed with other work, so after looking round the industry's consultants Triumph decided to give the task to the Karmann concern of West Germany.

Theirs was almost a 'mission impossible'. They were asked to produce a new body style, limited by the fact that much of the existing structure had to be retained, have it approved, and then to manufacture the new body tools, all in the space of about 14 months. That they did it is a credit to their speed of working, and to the fact that their first offering was approved.

Triumph insisted that the same *basic* body shell — floor, scuttle, screen, doors and inner panels — should be retained. Karmann could style a completely new nose and wings, and a new tail. The result, now so familiar on TR6s all over the world, looks very different but is very much more 'TR5' under the skin than might be apparent at a glance.

Karmann's style included a true full-width nose, with the headlamps at the extremities, and it also eliminated the oddity of a power-bulged bonnet where none was needed. The squared-off tail included a bit more luggage space than before, but a high rear sill which made access to the spare wheel a bit of a chore.

With all this came a new and angular one-piece optional hardtop (the old 'Surrey top' feature died with the TR5/TR250), which Triumph designed themselves without help from Karmann, and a few minor chassis changes. These included the use of wider wheel rims (5½in instead of 5in) and — at last — the provision of a front anti-roll bar.

The TR250 disappeared, as a separately badged model, and in its place the North American market began to receive cars simply

Wire wheels, as ever, were optional. To meet new United States legislation, there were massive side-lamps and indicators, with indicator repeaters ahead of the front wheel arches.

The TR6 was immediately recognizable from the tail with its new square-back style, the wrap-around tail-lamps and the transfer badges on the rear wings. The boot-lid was bigger than before, but the boot sill was substantially higher.

This shot of the 1970 model TR6, with its revised wheels, emphasizes the much wider rims — 5.5 inches — and the high-speed tyres with which they were matched. Along with the revised front-suspension geometry and the new front anti-roll bar this ensured that the TR6 handled better than the TR5.

The original version of the TR6's facia was identical to that of the TR5/TR250 except for the new steering wheel. The seats had been restyled, and now had 'breathing' covers.

called TR6s. They had missed out on the TR5s altogether, therefore, and they would never experience the delights of fuel-injected performance. A 'federal' TR6, called a TR6 Carb in factory shorthand, had the same 104bhp engine as before, and a performance just the same as the old TR250, or even the TR4A.

As with the previous models, 'federal' TRs were considered sufficiently different to have their own Commission Number sequence, so injected cars were all CP. . . . . ., while carburetted cars were CC. . . . . .

It would be very easy, of course, for an historian to suggest that the TR6 model then carried on basically unchanged until July 1976, when the very last car (Commission Number CF58328) rolled off the line in Coventry. It would also be true, but there were many significant detail updatings, all of which matter to a TR6 owner. The most important of these changes, as far as the customer was concerned, occured in the beginning of 1973 (autumn 1972 to the factory) when CR-series injected cars and CF-series carburetted cars took over from the old CP and CC models.

In regard to engines, I must describe the injection and the carburettor-engine changes separately. In the case of the injected engine, from 1969 to 1975 there were no obvious visible changes, and the only significant modification was to the camshaft, which was changed from a 35-65-65-35 degrees timing to the 18-58-58-18 degrees timing from the beginning of 1973 and the start up of the CR-series. This was done because there had been some customer complaints about the rather 'lumpy' traffic-driving characteristics of the very highly tuned 150bhp engine. In its final form the engine was smoother and more refined than before, but the power had slipped from 150bhp to an admittedly recalibrated 124bhp (DIN).

The TR6 'federal' engine struggled valiantly (and successfully) to keep within the ever-tightening exhaust-emission limits. Throughout its seven-year life it relied on Stromberg constant-vacuum carburettors to meter the fuel very accurately, with more and yet more equipment hung on downstream of the inlet manifolds to control the emission as the laws changed. Twin 175CDSE units were standard at first, then 175CDSE(2) units followed for 1971 and 1972, with 175CDSEV units for the last four years.

The fuel-injected engines used a 9.5:1 compression ratio throughout, but whereas the 'federal' engine started out with an 8.5:1 compression and a 10-50-50-10 degrees camshaft in 1969 (such as the TR250 had used), it was modified to a 7.75:1 ratio and the better-breathing 18-58-58-18 degrees camshaft from the start of the 1971 model year. The compression ratio drooped even further to 7.5:1 in 1975 and 1976, after which the car faded away, a mere shadow of its designers' true intentions.

For all this the USA-rated power held up remarkably well at about 105bhp, and even in its final strangulated form (except in California, where the limits applied were even more ludicrous) a TR6 Carb was about as fast as a TR4A had been. Towards the end, not only was there an exhaust gas recirculation system (exhaust gases, in part, being fed back into the inlet manifold), but also air injection by a pressure pump into the exhaust manifolds to help the combustion of unburnt hydrocarbons.

Between 1969 and 1976, too, there were two important transmission modifications which — rather confusingly — were not introduced at the same time. In the middle of 1971 the gearbox was changed, while from the start of the CR/CF-series an entirely new type of overdrive was used. At no time, however, was the final-drive ratio ever altered; all fuel-injected cars drove through a 3.45:1 differential, while all carburetted cars drove through a 3.7:1 ratio.

At first the TR6's gearbox was the same as that used in every TR4/TR4A/TR5/TR250 since 1961. Its internal ratios were 1.00, 1.33, 2.01, 3.24, and (reverse) 3.22:1. However, in June 1970 the very powerful Stag had been announced, with a stronger version of this gearbox and revised ratios. To rationalize the situation and to provide more built-in reserves of strength the TR6 inherited the same box, with internals of 1.00, 1.39, 2.10, 2.99 and 3.37:1. These ratios were marginally wider-spaced, but this was barely noticeable when the car was being driven normally.

The overdrive change was of more signficance. Ever since the first TR2s had been delivered a TR had been (optionally) equipped with the well-proven Laycock de Normanville 'A' Type overdrive, with its step-up ratio of 0.82:1. From the beginning of the 1973 model year, however, the much more modern 'J' Type was fitted, the step-up ratio of which was 0.797:1, and the wiring and cut-out switches on the top of the gearbox only allowed a 'J' Type to be used on top and third gears. As from the beginning of

For the first time since the arrival of the two-piece hardtop of 1961, for the TR4, a new hardtop option was made available for the TR. More angular than before, this TR6 extra was built in one piece and the rear quarter windows were fixed.

1973-model TR6s for the United States market had several minor cosmetic changes including the patriotic Union Jack badge incorporating the TR6 insignia. The seat headrests are just protruding above the sides of the open cockpit.

The front of the 1973-model TR6 was identified by the black plastic air-dam under the front bumper. This killed aerodynamic lift at high speeds and reduced drag under the car at the same time. A hidden improvement was the specification of the latest Laycock 'J' Type overdrive, which replaced the 'A' Type unit used ever since the earliest days of the 1953 TR2.

The TR6 as modified for 1973, with new steering wheel and differently-detailed instruments. In most respects, however, the facia was as designed for the TR5 in 1967, and much the same as that schemed by Michelotti in 1961 for the first TR4.

As United States legislation multiplied it became necessary to fit '5mph' bumpers which would protect the car in the case of a low-speed nose-tail shunt. These bulky over-riders were developed to meet the new laws.

A sad day for tradition, but not in the long term. The very last TR6 — destined for the United States — was built in Coventry in July 1976. All the TR7s, which replaced the TR6 series, were built at Liverpool, and at the time of writing the Coventry factory may cease the manufacture of complete cars altogether before long.

the 1974 model year, incidentally, the fitment of overdrive was standardized on the car.

Visually, and in detail, the TR6 came in for some attention during its life. At first, of course, it was introduced with the original TR5-type 'false' wheel trims, and many other carry-over trim items. From the autumn of 1969, starting conveniently from the Commission Number junction of 50,001, the cars were given new wheel trims, a new steering wheel with satin spokes, a matt-black surround to the screen to cut down reflections, and new seats which were claimed to be not only better shaped, but could also be adjusted for rake angle.

From the start of the 1973 model year — Commission Number series CR1 . . . . (injection) and CF1 . . . . . (carburettor) — the cars were given a new and very effective black plastic bib spoiler under the front bumper, satin-finish wheel trims, matt-black wiper blades and arms, a column-mounted headlamp dip-switch, differently-styled instruments, and (for North America) Union Jack rear wing transfers, including the TR6 insignia. When the new overdrive was considered, this was an important mid-term change.

This, however, was the end of serious development on the TR6 theme. Already the engineering department were hard at work on the development of yet another, entirely different, TR sports car, which it was planned to introduce, at least for the United States market, at the beginning of 1975.

Apart from the legislative work needed to keep the car abreast of the still-burgeoning North American safety laws, the TR6 coasted on towards retirement. In addition to details like the seat head-restraints (very obvious in profile when the car was being used with the hood down), the company also had to fit rather ugly but remarkably effective shock-absorbing over-riders (the '5mph bumpers' about which any safety engineer is apt to curse). One of the few important mechanical changes in this period was that the optional fitment of wire wheels was discontinued in May 1973 when demand had dropped to a low level.

Because the TR6 was finally assembled in Coventry, and because the new TR7 would be built entirely at Liverpool, there was to be no clean cut-off point from one model to another. The last fuel-injected TR6 was built in February 1975, but was price-listed in Britain to the end of that summer. Production of the 'federal' version, the TR6 Carb, carried on until the summer of 1976, with the very last being made in July. Even so, the last few sales did not take place until the beginning of 1977!

By then, of course, it was fashionable to knock the TR6 as an old design, but the fact is that even in 1975, when the customers had a choice of radically different TRs, they still chose to buy nearly 10,000 TR6s. Even so, in July 1976, we really did see the end of an era. The new TR7, which I describe fully in the next chapter, was all-new, with no carry-over parts from the TR6. The TR6, having sold nearly 95,000 examples, had done more for the factory than even the legendary TR3A.

When will we be able to say the same of the TR7?

CHAPTER 6

A new breed of TR

The TR7 range so far

When it was revealed in January 1975, the TR7 caused a great deal of controversy. This was not because it was a disappointment, but because it was so different from previous TRs. Sports car fans had, perhaps, been expecting a rugged and exciting car, something with the machismo they had come to know so well in old-style TRs. But the TR7 was absolutely new — a complete re-think.

In its philosophy the TR7 was such a new approach to two-seater motoring by Triumph that there were some people who thought it shouldn't be called a TR at all. I remember being involved in a confidential discussion way back in 1973 when I suggested that the new car should have a unique title — and offered 'Southern Cross' (a Triumph name from the distant past) as an idea. All manner of names, including the official adoption of 'Bullet' — which had been its experimental code name for so long — were canvassed, but in the end the simple TR7 title was chosen.

More so than any of its ancestors, the TR7 was laid out with export sales, particularly to North America, in mind. Sales figures so far published show that this approach must have been correct as more TR7s are being sold abroad than any previous TR has achieved. In 1976, for instance, more TR7s were exported than the TR3A ever achieved at the height of its fame, and when TR6 figures for 1976 are added, the total that year of 31,237 is half as many again as the TR3A's peak year of 1959!

The irony of all this is that an export-orientated design (aided by Leyland's marketing efforts) is selling better in Britain than any of its ancestors. More TR7s were sold at home in 1976 than ever before, and the 1977 statistics so far released show that even that figure has already been surpassed.

Therefore, in spite of what the diehards said when they first saw the design, it has already become a great success for Triumph and Leyland. More than 50,000 were built in less than three years — an unprecedented build rate; this might not be high by Detroit standards but it must be making Leyland's accountants very happy.

One thing should be made clear from the start. The TR7 is still a Triumph design. It is true that the styling is credited to the Austin-Morris studio at Longbridge, but the mechanical and body engineering was all carried out by the Triumph design team in Coventry. More than this, in spite of the company-wide rationalization which is forging ahead inside Leyland, all the major components are Triumph-designed.

Even so, for Triumph the TR7 is a completely new approach to sports-car design. Let me compare it, for instance, with the TR6. The TR7 was engineered as a hardtop coupe instead of an open car, with unit body-chassis construction in place of a separate chassis frame, with a live axle instead of independent rear suspension, with MacPherson front struts instead of a wishbone linkage, and — most surprising of all — with a four-cylinder engine instead of a 'six'.

Nothing was carried over and the TR7 was even built in a different factory at first. Final assembly was at Speke, Liverpool, but after the long strike of 1977-78 body build went to a Pressed Steel Fisher plant in the Midlands and TRs were assembled at Coventry. There was another move in 1980, when assembly was transferred to Rover's plant at Solihull.

BL's intention to offer a whole family of TR7s was delayed by

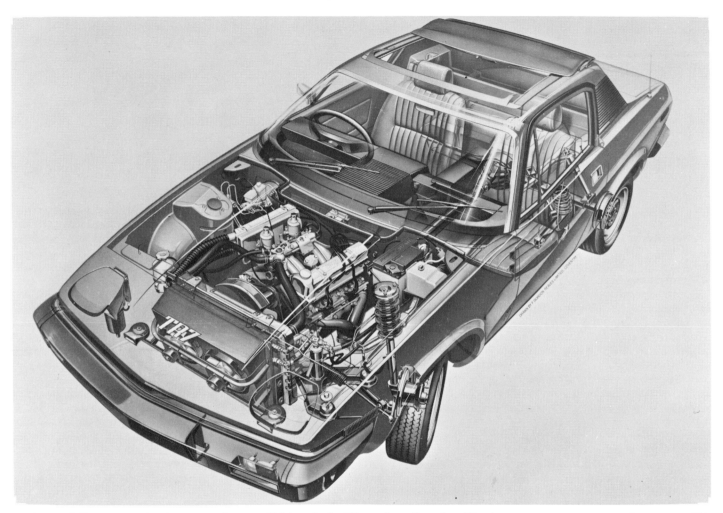

A 'ghosted' TR7, demonstrating the compact layout, which is radically different from all previous TRs; there are no carry-over parts of any nature. This version is that sold for the non-federal markets, and is made with left-hand or right-hand drive. Cars intended for the United States (all left-hand drive) are fitted with less powerful and extensively de-toxed engines (the kit includes a catalytic converter in the exhaust system), and even more robust '5mph' bumpers. At the time of writing there is no convertible option to the fixed-head TR7, though one has been rumoured for the future. Front suspension is by MacPherson struts, and the rear-axle beam is located by coil springs and radius arms. The engine is closely related to the eight-valve 1,854cc units fitted to Triumph Dolomite saloons since 1972. There is an engine-driven viscous cooling fan, and the electric radiator fans shown are part of the optional air-conditioning kit.

The TR7's wheels have simple four-bolt fixings with exposed wheel nuts, and radial-ply tyres are standard. This is a non-federal car, which can be recognized by the lack of flashing indicator repeaters above the corners of the front bumper and in the rear wings near the tail; decorative blanks are fitted in their place. The headlamps can be raised electrically by controls in the driving compartment. The engine air intake is under the bumper. Since mid-1977, a sun-roof option has been available.

This is an excuse for introducing Sue Cuff (ex-Miss Great Britain and one of Leyland's favourite models); she is leaning on the 1977 version of the TR7, which has different suspension settings, sits rather lower on the road, and has brighter interior fittings and more equipment to match its revised wheel-trims.

the strike. A 16-valve 'Sprint' version was actually in preproduction when the strike began, but was abandoned during the move. The pretty convertible was also strike-bound, but finally went on sale in the USA in mid-1979 and in Britain in 1980. The important Rover vee-8-engined TR8, also strike-bound, was rallied by Abingdon from 1978 and went on sale in America in 1980. No more was heard of the long-wheelbase 'Lynx' coupe which was to have replaced the Stag. BL Heritage still have the abandoned prototypes.

Work on a new Triumph TR began almost as soon as the TR6 had been finalized. I describe the thinking behind new schemes in the next chapter, and give illustrations of the way Coventry's engineers and stylists were thinking. The fact that the British Leyland merger and its after-effects made these original schemes fruitless is a pity, but this could not hide what Triumph had already decided — that there was no scope for yet another design on the generation-old layout of TRs. Any new sports car really would be new, from end to end.

To design a new engine and a new transmission for the car made no economic sense, which meant that Triumph would have to look round the corporation for their major 'building blocks', but at least they would not be hampered by an existing chassis, nor by the basics of an existing pressed-steel body.

Their work with the 'Fury' prototype had already shown that an open-topped car with unit construction was perfectly feasible. The body assembly facility at the vastly-expanded Triumph factory at Liverpool was well used to this form of body-shell (they also built the Toledo/1500/Dolomite shells, and that of the Stag Grand Touring car).

At the project stage there was much discussion about the car's basic configuration. At the end of the 1960's British Leyland were still convinced that they could finance many more projects than they later found to be practical. At this time, for instance, Triumph were asked to put up proposals for a conventional front-engined sports car, while their MG rivals at Abingdon were invited to design a mid-engined car around the Austin Maxi and 2200 power packs. Not that anything was decided as simply as that; Triumph were also interested in the idea of a mid-engined car, and went to some lengths to canvass their North American sales organization and some of the more influential motoring magazines on the subject. The fact that alternative wheelbases were thought of (see Chapter 7), and that more than two seats might be necessary, made Triumph plump for a classic front-engine layout.

In the car's general structural layout the North American safety legislation (real or merely threatened) has much to answer for. At the design stage it looked perfectly obvious that convertible cars would soon be outlawed in the United States (proposed crash/roll-over regulations were an important factor), and so the new 'Bullet' was laid out as a closed car. This enabled Triumph to build in enormous strength to the screen pillars and the rear quarters, while the roof panel added to the shell's general rigidity.

For the same reasons there are beams inside the doors (to resist side intrusion in mandatory tests), and vast, complex and expensive bumpers, front and rear, to comply with the 'no body damage in 5mph accidents' legislation. The whole structure is heavier and even stronger than commonsense and years of experience suggest is necessary, but try telling that to the legislators in Washington DC. The fact that these strong bumpers often cause more damage in some areas than they save in others, and are very expensive to replace, cuts no ice either!

The MacPherson-strut front suspension and the live rear axle located by radius arms and sprung on coil springs are both unique to the TR7, although this was not originally intended. Many suspension parts were to have been shared with a new medium-sized Triumph car, of which prototypes were actually built, but this project was cancelled in the aftermath of British Leyland's financial collapse and the reorganization according to the Ryder Report. Both the front and the rear suspension have an anti-roll bar, that at the rear being bolted to the trailing location arms, and rack-and-pinion steering is specified.

As with previous TRs, so with the TR7, the engine and transmission are all basically standard Triumph items modified and improved specifically to suit the TR7's requirements. Basically the engine is shared with the Dolomite saloons (and in parentage with the Saab 99 and Stag vee-8 engines), the four-speed gearbox with the Marina/Triumph 1500TC/Dolomite/Spitfire/MG Midget, and the axle with various other small Triumph saloons, including the Dolomite. But in each case there are important improvements.

The engine has no links with the TR's past. It was originally laid down in the early 1960's as part of a new family — a

When a long strike closed the TR7 Speke factory in the winter of 1977-78, the first series of convertible TR7s were locked in, partly built, and announcement of this very pretty derivative was delayed until mid-1979 (for North America) and until March 1980 (for Britain and the rest of the world). Body sheet-metal changes were confined to those necessitated by the use of a folding hood — the car is arguably much sleeker in this guise. The vee-8-engined TR8 is also sold with this open body style. This view emphasizes that a TR7 is a much more compact car than the TR6 which it replaced.

Announced in January 1975, the federal version of the TR7 had this interior. The seats had brushed nylon facings, and there was a big pad over the centre of the steering wheel to meet United States safety requirements.

Apart from the right-hand drive in this picture, the non-federal TR7s revealed in May 1976 could only be distinguished by the different detailing of the steering wheel spokes. The big grilles in the centre of the door trim pads hide the loudspeakers for the radio or other I.C.E. equipment. The radio, when fitted, lives in a pouch between the heater controls, but an open oddments box is standard.

Part of the 1977 package of revisions includes these smart tartan seat facings. There are no mechanical changes from the original TR7.

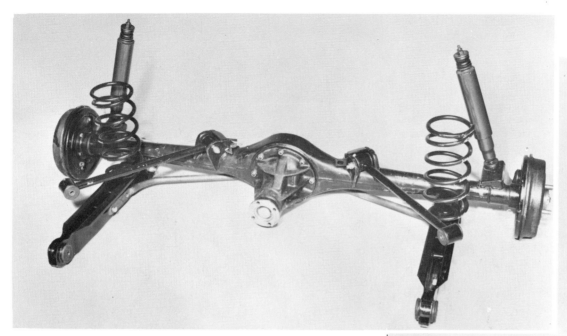

After being equipped with independent rear suspension for ten years, the TR pedigree reverted to a beam axle for the TR7. This is a corporate unit, the design being shared with the Triumph Dolomite range and other cars in the Leyland line-up, but the coil spring and radius-arm linkage geometry was developed specially for the TR7. There is a stout anti-roll bar connecting the lower radius arms, but a recent Triumph 'trade mark' is the large amount of wheel movement, with soft coil springs and progressive damper settings. This is the axle assembly normally fitted to TR7s with the four-speed gearbox. The heavy-duty axle, based on the design of the new Rover 3500 unit, comes with bigger rear drum brakes, and is allied to the optional five-speed gearbox.

The TR7's front suspension (right) looks strange to traditional TR fans. There is a stout pressed-steel cross-member which bolts to the unit-construction shell, a bottom 'wishbone' comprising one transverse link and the actuating arm of the anti-roll bar, and a MacPherson strut combining a telescopic damper with a coil spring, which is fixed to the body-shell at the top of the inner wheel-arch. Steering is by rack-and-pinion, and the disc brakes are vacuum servo-assisted.

four-cylinder unit inclined at 45 degrees in the chassis and a corresponding vee-8. The four-cylinder units were first revealed in the Saab 99 and were delivered to them from Coventry in large quantities; for some years, however, Saab have taken over the complete manufacture of their version of the design.

The engine has a single overhead camshaft, and an in-line row of inclined valves. In original Saab guise it displaced 1,709cc, and for the Dolomite it is still 1,854cc. However, when the special Dolomite Sprint engine was developed, with its clever 16-valve cylinder-head, the capacity was stretched to 1,998cc, with a bore of 90.3mm and a stroke of 78mm.

A special variant of the engine was developed for the TR7. While the capacity of 1,998cc and its attendant bore and stroke are familiar, this 'bottom end' has been matched to the original single-camshaft eight-valve cylinder-head. In effect, then, a TR7 engine is an amalgam of Dolomite 1850 and Dolomite Sprint, and is one not yet found on any other Leyland car.

Because the TR7 sells so widely in North America there has to be two very different versions of this engine. The two are easily spotted externally — the 'federal' unit being fuelled by twin Stromberg 175CD SEV carburettors, nearly hidden under a maze of extra piping, while the rest of the world sees twin horizontal SU HS6 instruments allied to a much cleaner and neater engine.

The 'federal' engine is also burdened by exhaust gas recirculation and air injection into the exhaust ports. There is also a charcoal canister to absorb evaporative emissions from the carburettors and the fuel system. The compression ratio is 8.0:1, the engine can run on non-leaded fuel, and it produces about 92bhp at 5,000rpm. In this form, in certain climatic conditions, the TR7's driveability is not pleasant, but it does at least meet the incredibly strict exhaust emission limits demanded in the United States.

So it seems that after 25 years of producing successful TR sports cars the wheel has turned full circle, with the same sort of power produced as with the TR2's 'agricultural' wet-liner Vanguard-type engine! Perhaps the 1977 breed of horses are a little tougher than they were so long ago because the rather heavier TR7 performs in almost the same way as did the TR2, with equally promising fuel economy potential. But it can give no sort of pleasure to the designers to have to sell a car to the TR enthusiast which really hasn't advanced all that much, and which

This display-cutaway TR7 engine is in federal guise, complete with Zenith-Stromberg carburettors and the pipework and mass of extra fittings needed to eliminate exhaust emissions.

is 250 pounds heavier into the bargain.

Fortunately for the rest of the world, 'their' TR7 is an altogether faster and more interesting machine. Not only is it slightly lighter and shorter than that sent to North America, but the engine is not hung about with all kinds of power-throttling equipment. The compression ratio is up to 9.25:1, and maximum power of 105bhp (DIN) is developed at 5,500rpm. A combination of 14 per cent more power in two per cent less weight makes for a much more spritely performance, which shows up well in independent road-testing figures. In all but flat-out tyre-screeching acceleration a TR7 can hold a TR6, and since figures were never taken on the post-1973 version of the TR6 it is likely that the new car matches *that* one in all respects.

It is true that maximum speed is down — back to just under

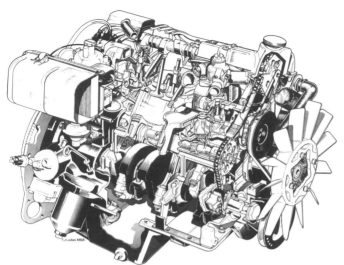

A splendidly detailed cutaway of the TR7's 2-litre single-overhead-camshaft engine. The block, and the line of the cylinders, is angled over at 45 degrees towards the left side of the car. This is a non-federal version complete with twin SU carburettors. Federal versions have specially set tamper-proof Zenith-Stromberg units, and much related equipment to minimize exhaust emissions. The United States TR7s, therefore, and especially those sold in California, are much slower than those built for the rest of the world. The parentage of this engine goes back to a design jointly developed for Saab (the 99 series) and for Triumph (the Dolomite). There is also the vee-8 3-litre Stag derivative, and the even more important 16-valve 1,998cc engine already specified for the Dolomite Sprint.

In-car installation of the non-federal TR7 eight-valve engine, identified by its SU carburettors and its clean and uncluttered appearance. At bottom left is the optional air-conditioning pump, and the direct-acting brake servo to bottom right indicates that this is a left-hand-drive car. The bonnet, like that of all TRs made after 1961, is hinged at the front. The rubber bungs and the pressed-steel towers at each side of the engine hide the top fixings for the front suspension's MacPherson struts.

Optional on the TR7 from an early stage was the all-new five-speed gearbox, in which fourth gear was the direct ratio and fifth an 'overdrive' gear. From outside the car there is no way of identifying the fitting of this box, and inside the cockpit the gear knob markings are the only giveaway.

This is a cutaway demonstration assembly of the TR7's five-speed gearbox. Called the '77mm' box (the dimension is the spacing between the mainshaft and layshaft centres), it is shared with the very fast new Rover 3500 and is extremely strong.

110mph (a figure which only the fuel-injected TR5s and TR6s ever beat) — but fuel economy is substantially improved; most owners record 27 to 30mpg, which is a pleasant reversion to something approaching TR3/TR3A days.

The transmission line-up is a bit complicated, particularly as some of the options have changed. As originally announced, and still listed as the 'base' equipment, the car had an 8.5in diaphragm-spring clutch and an all-synchromesh four-speed gearbox which had a single-rail selector mechanism, and whose basic design was already in use in several other British Leyland models. An optional overdrive was not listed, though this could certainly have been provided if required as the same gearbox is built with overdrive for the Dolomite saloon, and the original TR7 works rally cars used overdrive transmissions under the same floor pan for their first few events. The box itself has torque limitations, and for more powerful versions of the TR7 there are alternative arrangements, described below.

Unlike the TR6, the TR7 has a live axle and reveals nothing in common with previous TR equipment. The old TR2/3/4 axle was derived from Vanguard/Mayflower engineering, while the TR4A/5/250/6 differential was chassis-mounted and leaned heavily on the Triumph 2000 for its bits and pieces. The TR7's axle has a differential shared with the Dolomite 1850, the Spitfire and the Morris Marina 1.8, while the axle case has much in common with that of the Dolomite 1850 and the Marina.

Transmission complications set in when we consider options. In place of an optional overdrive to raise the gearing Triumph now offer a complete gearbox transplant — a five-speed all-synchromesh unit of the type first seen in the Rover 3500 and since offered in the six-cylinder Rover 2300 and 2600 models. This effectively provides an overdrive because the 'direct' top gear is fourth, and fifth has a step-up ratio of 0.833:1. The Rover gearbox, known as the '77mm' box inside the factory because this is the spacing between the mainshaft and layshaft centres, is much stronger than the basic four-speed box and is an obvious candidate for standardization behind the more powerful TR7 variants when these are announced.

Fifth gear is obviously meant to be used as an overdrive as the gear-change gate is arranged that way; while first to fourth are in the usual H-layout, fifth is found in a slot to the right of the main gate.

The first of the five-speed cars came down the Liverpool assembly line towards the end of 1975, but they were not revealed publicly until the autumn of 1976. For reasons already stated (and to rationalize further with future versions of the TR7) the five-speed car has always been supplied with the bigger, stronger and heavier back axle, which includes a 3.9:1 differential, and it has much bigger rear brakes.

Another transmission option made available at the same time as the five-speed manual gearbox was automatic transmission — for the first time ever on a TR. For the United States it has been available since 1975. As I have already mentioned, prototypes with automatic gearboxes had been built on several occasions, but until the 1970's it was never thought necessary to put them on the market. In the case of the TR7, the Borg-Warner three-speed Type 65 gearbox was chosen — a proprietory unit used widely in British and European cars and one with great reserves of strength and an excellent reputation for reliability. In this case a 3.27:1 axle ratio was specified along with the original light-duty axle casing. That ratio, incidentally, had already seen Triumph use in the GT6, the Dolomite 1500 and the Dolomite 1850 — I mention this to show how the 'building block' mentality is now well-developed in the Leyland design process.

The TR7, like other TRs, has front-wheel disc brakes (9.7in front discs) and rear-wheel drums (8 x 1.5in drums on the light-duty axle, 9 x 1.75in on the medium-duty axle), along with a direct-acting brake servo and dual hydraulic circuits. At this stage there is no choice of wheels — all TR7s are built with pressed-steel disc wheels having 5½-in rims. The base car has 175-13in radial-ply tyres, while the 'medium-duty' specification includes 185/70-13in covers.

Apart from the mechanical specification, which was new throughout, it was necessary for a TR enthusiast to come to terms with the TR7's facia and interior. For the first time the traditional layout of instruments — traditional, that is, since Walter Belgrove's team had designed the TR1 back in 1952 — was abandoned, and an ultra-modern arrangement was provided which included neatly integrated positioning of the ventilation system, the optional air conditioning, the radio and other extras.

This time there was absolutely no space behind the seats, unlike in the older TRs where soft luggage, dogs or even consenting children could be housed for reasonable journeys. With the TR7

In works rallying guise, the TR7 is not only much more powerful and even stronger than when standard, but has a bright corporate colour scheme, and usually a battery of extra halogen driving lamps (they are covered here by protective 'tea cosies' to protect the lenses from stone damage).

Even before the end of its first rallying season the TR7s were becoming competitive with far more specialized machines and had started to win. To obtain this performance they were fitted with highly developed 16-valve versions of the 1,998cc engine, which was not then a TR7 production-line fitting, but was readily available as it was standard on the Dolomite Sprint.

The works rally cars have a stark and purposeful interior with special small-diameter steering wheel, gear-lever knob including an overdrive switch (in 1976 the five-speed box had not been made available) and special seats. The standard rev counter has been replaced by a special competition unit from Smiths.

An early version of the TR7 16-valve rally engine, showing the twin double-choke Weber carburettors which the regulations permit.

BL Motorsport, at Abingdon, began using TR7V8 rally cars in 1978, nearly two years before the production car was launched in North America as the TR8. At first it was a difficult rough-surface car to drive, but it was always competitive on tarmac, and *always* fast enough. Tony Pond drove this car to a fine outright win in the 24 Hours of Ypres rally in 1978.

Since the TR7 had always been designed with the 3½-litre Rover vee-8 engine in mind, conversion of the works rally cars from 'fours' was a simple job for Abingdon to perform. The first cars used a simple carburettor installation featuring two twin-choke Webers feeding a common manifold, and disposing of between 285 and 300bhp. A Pierburg fuel-injection system was tried once, in 1979, but the definitive TR7V8s of 1980 usually had four horizontal twin-choke Webers and produced well over 300bhp at 7,500rpm, and no less than 245lb ft of torque at 5,500rpm.

seats pushed all the way back there was no gap in front of the bulkhead hiding the petrol tank, and the only stowage space was on shaped trays in front of the rear window.

TR spotters no doubt enjoy identifying a 'federal' TR7 from the rest-of-the-world variety; it is identified by its more massive bumpers (including the built-in over-riders), by the indicator repeater lamps in the rear wings, and by the modified fuel-filler cap which will only accept the nozzle of a 'non-leaded' fuel pump. The specially-padded steering wheel is another clue, and under the bonnet there is just no way of mistaking the spider's web of extra wiring and tubing which any comprehensively de-toxed engine needs these days.

None of these facts and figures, however, can describe the incredible advances made in roadholding and handling. When he was technical chief at Triumph, Spencer King introduced a new philosophy of providing cars with soft suspension and lengthy wheel travel. In this way it became clear that a really well sorted and located live rear axle could perform as well as most independent suspensions, and the TR7 proves this point. Its response, its ride and its handling is a great improvement over any previous TR, and sets new standards by which all new Triumphs will have to be judged.

In Britain, incidentally, the position regarding the optional five-speed transmission has been rather confused. Announced in the autumn of 1976, the option was withdrawn in the spring of 1977 and it is no coincidence that at the same time the five-speed box became a '100 per cent' fitment for the very important 'federal' market. The problem, particularly regarding the medium-duty axle, is purely one of supply and demand, and the situation at the time of writing is that the fortunate British owner of a five-speed TR7 has something akin to a collector's item.

If the TR7 had been more successful in its early years, additional model derivatives would have been added to fill out the range more quickly. The one really crippling mishap was the *four-month* strike by bloody-minded and suicidal workers, which closed down the Speke factory just as the new models were beginning to flow down the lines. The hiatus — which, with other non-related stoppages, meant that few TR7s were built between September 1977 and October 1978 — meant that some models were never produced at all and others were much delayed.

Without the stoppage, the 1978 range would definitely have seen the introduction of a 16-valve (Dolomite Sprint)-engined version of the car, to be called a TR7 Sprint, a 3,528cc Rover vee-8-engined car, to be called the TR8, and the option of a sleek convertible body as an alternative to the fixed-head coupe introduced in 1975. In addition to all this, the Stag vee-8 had been dropped in June 1977, and its successor was to have been another development on the TR7 theme, a vee-8-engined (Rover, not Stag engine, by the way) car with a 12-inch longer wheelbase, and a startlingly attractive fastback coupe body with nose, front wings and screen from the TR7 and a rear-end style rather reminiscent of the Lotus Eclat. At Triumph, this car was codenamed 'Lynx'.

None of this, incidentally, is conjecture. On a guided tour of the deserted Speke lines in the autumn of 1977, I saw the Sprint, the TR8 and the convertible bodies all marooned in the workshops, and the redundant Stag facilities had been cleared away ready for 'Lynx' tooling to be installed.

The Speke dispute was temporarily settled in March 1978 *after* BL's new chairman, Michael Edwardes, had confirmed that it was to be closed-off, but TR7 production finally came to an end in May. There was then a six-month hiccup while the body-tooling facilities were transferred to BL's Pressed Steel Fisher factory at Swindon and the partly-finished left-overs were moved down to the Coventry factory, while the necessary rejigging and retraining went ahead. Production was resumed in October 1978, with the five-speed gearbox as standard.

The Sprint model was never released, though the preproduction cars (25, reputedly) were sold off. The convertible was finally introduced to North America in summer 1979, and became available in Britain in March 1980, but in each case only with the eight-valve four-cylinder engine.

At last, the Rover-engined TR8 was launched in the USA at the beginning of 1980, but at the time these words were written it had not been marketed in Britain. It is a convertible, with broader wheels and a slightly different bonnet pressing, but is otherwise virtually indistinguishable from the four-cylinder car.

There was a further complication in 1980 when, in an effort to rationalize Rover-Triumph production (and cut costs), all assembly of cars at Canley was terminated and TR7/TR8 assembly was moved once again — this time to the Rover factory at Solihull, where it continued until late-1981.

CHAPTER 7

Prototypes and specials

Zoom, Italia, Francorchamps and others

Like any other active car maker, over the years Triumph have designed several more models than have ever been produced in quantity. In the case of the TRs, too, there have been a few special-bodied creations which reached the market in small numbers. Most of the prototypes were eventually sold off, and most have been preserved. This brings history into the present, and helps to fill out the missing links in the TR's pedigree.

To be a Triumph prototype expert you have to talk in terms of code names. A 'Zoom' is quite different from a 'Zest', a 'Fury' from a 'Lynx', and each name was applied to a particular product. A few names, as I have already indicated, were hived off by an official 'TR' model when they reached production — 'Zest' becoming TR4, 'Wasp' becoming TR5, and 'Bullet' the TR7.

The original classic shape ran from 1953 to 1962, as TR2, TR3, TR3A and finally TR3B. This does not, however, mean that the factory had no intention of changing the car in the meantime; demand was such that they had no need to do so.

There were attempts to revise and up-date the TR2/TR3, even in the mid-1950s, but these never progressed beyond the sketch stages. Apart from the Francorchamps variant, described later, nothing came to fruition, and it was Giovanni Michelotti from Turin (with Vignale actually building the car) who produced the first complete restyle.

This was an ultra-fashionable machine, later dubbed the 'Dream Car', with full-width styling, straight-through wing lines, pronounced tail fins and a gaping Detroit-style radiator grille. Registered VHP 720, it first took to the road in 1957, and was used by Triumph's managing director Alick Dick for about a year. *The Autocar* tried the car in the summer of 1958, pointed

out firmly that it was not a prototype but more of an ideas car, and it disappeared into limbo.

Michelotti, in the meantime, had become contracted to Triumph, and was asked to develop a completely new body-shell for fitment to a modified TR3/TR3A chassis frame. It was not at all a simple brief because there were two variables to be considered — a change in wheel tracks to improve roadholding, space and looks, and an increase in wheelbase to make provision for the twin-cam 2-litre 20X engine (already described in Chapter 4).

Michelotti's first effort was on an unmodified TR chassis, with its familiar 7ft 4in wheelbase and the 3ft 9in tracks. Even at that time it was coded 'Zest', and in its side view and general layout it was like the TR4, but looking considerably narrower. This car was built in the winter of 1957-58, but not registered until the autumn of 1958. It could be used either as a soft-top sports car, or as a coupe, when a Triumph Herald coupe roof was employed, and there was a forward-facing scoop in the bonnet to feed cold air to the carburettors. This car, incidentally, had the chassis number X614 and was sold off by the factory in 1962.

Providing for the longer twin-cam 20X engines led to another project, the 'Zoom', of which two examples were made. These cars had lines in side view very much like those of the 1958 'Zest', but with the six inches added to the wheelbase (between the front wheels and the front doors, so there was no benefit in passenger space) and with the 4ft 1in wheel tracks which eventually were standardized on the TR4.

Zooms had hot-air outlets above and behind the front wheel-arches, headlamps conventionally positioned at the nose of the front wings, and simple full-width radiator grilles. Coded X644 and X655, and registered YKV 259 and YKV 260, respectively, these cars were built in 1959 and were fitted from the outset with detuned twin-cam 20X engines.

Their body shapes, as I have already made clear, were duplicated by the second-generation TRS Le Mans cars raced in 1960 and 1961, those of course being constructed of glass-fibre. From the scuttle backwards, the body style and engineering was almost identical with that of the production TR4s. Both cars were sold off when the decision to drop the long-wheelbase project had been taken. One of them, at least, is now undergoing restoration in Great Britain. It is obvious from the present owner's information that it was sold by the factory with a normal TR3A/TR4 engine instead of the twin-cam.

The proper TR4, still coded 'Zest' at that stage, evolved as a combination of ideas from the 1957-58 'Zest' and the 'Zooms'. A widened nose style from the first car (WDU 708), complete with the now-familiar inset headlamps, was grafted on to the centre and rear sections of the 'Zoom'. The first of these cars — X664, registered 9132 HP — was built early in 1961 and it was not until this point in the development story that the two-piece hardtop scheme was produced.

In 1960 and 1961, however, the Standard-Triumph group were in all manner of financial difficulties. Money needed to tool-up a TR4 body-shell was hard to find, and as an alternative it was proposed that the widened chassis should be slotted under a TR3A body modified only with bulbous front and rear wings to cover the pushed-out wheels. Two of these cars, variously called TR3Bs and even 'Betas', were built and could be distinguished only by modified radiator grilles, fatter wings, and direction indicator/sidelamps on these wings instead of in the TR3A grille position. One of them — X662 — was scrapped, but X693 was sold off and is still in existence.

Also in the 1950's, a TR3A was built-up with Borg-Warner automatic transmission and later sold off, reputedly converted back to standard, and one all-independent 'lash-up' was made, but this was later scrapped.

TR4 evolved into TR4A with the minimum of diversions, except that as already mentioned the factory proposed to give the TR4A a final stretch of the old engine to 2,499cc with a 93mm

The TR 'Dream Car' commissioned by Alick Dick as Michelotti's first styling job on the TR3. This car was never seriously intended for production, but was an 'ideas' project. Thought to be very smart and fashionable when built in 1957, its hooded headlamps dated quickly, but the full-width grille pre-dated that of the TR3A and inspired that change. Even so, its fixed screen and the wind-up windows were pointers to the future TR4, even if the colour scheme and the tail fins were not.

As an interim car between the TR3A and the TR4, this TR3 'Beta', of which only two were built, was seriously proposed for production. Not to be confused with the few thousand TR3Bs which *were* built in 1961-62, the 'Beta' combined the basic TR3A body-shell with the wide-track TR4 chassis and rack-and-pinion steering. From this view the special radiator grille is the sole identification feature . . .

. . . but from head-on the fatter wing pressings, to adequately cover the wider-spaced wheels, are obvious.

The Triumph Italia was a series-production car with a TR3A chassis and a Michelotti-styled but Vignale-built coupe body-shell, built by Vignale between 1959 and 1963. As originally shown in 1958, in prototype guise, it had a drooping nose and hidden headlamps, but it was always sold with the style illustrated here. The coachbuilt bodies were made entirely of steel, and a handful were imported to Britain. It was a very smart, though expensive coupe, which unfortunately could not be built at the right price in Britain.

The Italia had the characteristic Vignale crossed flags on the rear wings and was badged, prophetically enough, as a 'Triumph 2000'!

Michelotti's first efforts to fulfil his brief for the 'Zest' project. This particular car — a one-off prototype — used the unwidened TR3A chassis with an all-new steel body. Although it was considerably narrower than the TR4 which went into production, many of the styling features show a resemblance; the front grille, the hooded headlamps and the general proportions are all familiar. The author once took this car to a motor club meeting shortly after the TR4's announcement and confused a great number of people! The removable hardtop on this prototype was lifted directly from a Triumph Herald Coupe.

From this angle the Herald Coupe roof-line is more obvious, and the proposed rearward position of the fuel tank (and the filler cap near the tail) is also obvious on the original 1958 'Zest' prototype.

'Zoom' was a very serious attempt to produce the style for a new TR4. There were two 'Zoom' prototypes — YKV 259 and YKV 260 — both having the six-inch increase in wheelbase and the four-inch track increases proposed for a new model. This extra length was provided between the front wheels and the driving compartment and was to accommodate the longer twin-cam 'Sabrina' 20X engine. A visual difference between the two prototypes is that one had hot-air vents in the wings behind the front wheels; they also had different sill details. These cars produced the body shape for the 1960-61 TRS Le Mans cars and led to the definitive TR4 'Zests'. From the windscreen backwards the shape of the production TR4 was nearly the same as that of the 'Zooms', while the final nose and front wings had much in common with Michelotti's 1958 'Zest'.

Proof that the 20X twin-cam was seriously considered as a production option. A de-tuned (about 120bhp) version of 20X was installed in this 'Zoom' prototype, using twin SU carburettors.

If the Le Mans programme had been continued for 1962 it is highly likely that this very special version of the TRS, described in Chapter 4, would have been used. Styling was by Michelotti, and the whole machine was built in Italy by Conrero, the ace engine tuner.

This view of the Conrero TRS shows the swept tail, the boot (which was required by Le Mans 24-hours race regulations) and the vast fuel-filler cap let into the rear window.

The Conrero TRS's engine was unique in that it was fitted with twin double-choke Weber carburettors.

The no-nonsense interior and facia of the Conrero-TRS Le Mans project.

'Fury' — the first-ever monocoque sporting Triumph. Only one was built, and it is now in private hands. It featured all-independent suspension and a modified Triumph 2000 six-cylinder engine. It was really one size down from the existing TR sports cars.

cylinder bore and a dry-liner cylinder block, but this was never put into production.

In the meantime, as a gap-filler between the forthcoming TR5 and the little Spitfire, a new project was designed in 1964-65 called the 'Fury'. It was a curious amalgam of ideas, with an open two-seater unit-construction body-shell, a body style by Michelotti with a definite relationship to Spitfire, and mechanical parts from both TR4A and Triumph 2000. 'Fury' had all-independent suspension, entirely special to this project — MacPherson-strut coil springs at the front, and semi-trailing links with coil springs at the rear.

The engine was a tuned 2-litre six-cylinder Triumph 2000 unit, the gearbox identical with that of the TR4A, and the body-mounted axle unit was also from the TR4A. It had centre-lock wire wheels, and the sleek styling included pop-up headlamps and a squared-off tail, the theme of which was later used on all the Triumphs of the late 1960's.

Completed in 1965, it was used by the factory until 1968, then sold. It has passed through various hands, and is now owned by John Ward of Bromsgrove. Its registration number now (GL 484) is a personalized one, and its original number (TVT 990G) was taken out by the Triumph dealership in Staffordshire who bought it from the factory. In the marketing scheme of things, the GT6 was built and sold instead.

It is worth recalling that several 'mock-up' attempts were made to develop a TR4B, or 'Wasp', one quite a successful one with a lengthened nose and lengthened tail, before TR5 eventually went into production as virtually a re-engined TR4A.

TR6 followed on swiftly from TR5, with Karmann making the tools and doing the styling job. To succeed TR6, and in a way to supplement Stag, the factory then began to think about a new family of cars. By 1968-69, two distinct cars were evolving — a two-seater car coded 'Bullet', and a two-plus-two derivative of it coded 'Lynx'. Bullet, as already detailed, eventually became the current TR7. The two cars would be mechanically similar, and were intended to share some common engineering and pressed-steel body panels under the skin, but would look completely different.

Triumph's own proposal for the TR7 body style, here seen in full-size mock-up guise. It was later superseded by the Longbridge-shaped TR7 which we know so well. This one never progressed beyond the mock-up stage.

You have to look carefully at the size of the grass underfoot to realize that these are quarter-scale mock-ups of two proposed new Triumphs. In 1969 the factory were considering making two related cars in the future — a two-seater TR7 (with the '1973' and 'Bullet' plates shown), and a two-plus-two-seater (plated as '1972' and 'Lynx'). The badging and the details are interesting, but the entire philosophy was upset by the onset of Rover-Triumph in 1972, and later by the formation of Leyland Cars in 1975. Triumph's future policy will have nothing in common with these ideas, pleasant though they were.

One special version of the TR4, not factory-sponsored, was this GTR4 Dové, built by Harringtons and sold by the Triumph distributors Dove of Wimbledon. There was angular fastback styling, with a repositioned petrol tank, but the chassis was not changed. Its only fault was that it was too expensive — nevertheless, it pre-dated the MGB GT by a couple of years.

The TR2 Francorchamps, of which just 22 were built by the Triumph Belgian importers. Mechanically the cars were absolutely standard, and the fixed steel hardtops included a plexiglass panel in the roof. The door panels were built up and wind-up window glasses specified. Those 'wire' wheels were false and rather unsuitable trims over the usual disc wheels.

Back in 1969, though, the factory's first priority was the bigger 'Lynx', which they wanted to launch in 1972. In 1969 and 1970 no fewer than six prototypes of this car were built, but before planning could go any further ahead, rationalization within British Leyland became vital and the 'Lynx' project was cancelled.

'Bullet', of course, prospered, and with the help of Longbridge stylists the familiar two-seater coupe shape was finalized by the end of 1971. The TR7 family, as we have seen, is still growing fast, and will certainly out-date this book in due course.

Two versions of the TR2/TR3 and one version of the TR4 went into small-scale production and should be mentioned here. Chronologically, the Coupe Francorchamps came first. This was a permanent hardtop version of the TR2/TR3 body, as re-engineered by Imperia (in Nessonvaux, Belgium) who were Triumph's Belgian importers. Mechanically there were no changes, and the body-shell was still recognizably TR2, but the doors were built up so that wind-up windows could be fitted. The hardtop swept down to the cut-out line of the cockpit, and was complete with plexiglass 'sun roof' and rear window. Fixed quarter windows were added in front of and behind the door glasses. I understand that only 22 were made in all, in 1954 and 1955.

A more successful and comprehensive conversion was Vignale's Triumph Italia, a very smart two-seater fixed-head coupe styled by Michelotti and fitted to a TR3A chassis. When first seen at the Turin Show in 1958 it had a drooping nose with faired-in headlamps and a radiator inlet hidden under the front bumper. On entering production in 1959 (at about one car a day) it had a conventional nose and grille not unlike but *not* the same as the 'Zoom'. The Italia was certainly much more expensive than a TR3A, even though a very graceful car. In Italy it cost £1,440 compared with £1,140 for a TR3A.

The bodies, incidentally, were coachbuilt but in steel, and of the several hundred built only a dozen or so were in right-hand-drive form. The back-axle ratio, incidentally, was 4.3 to 1, and overdrive was a standard fitting on the first cars, but later machines were built with the normal TR3A mechanical specification. The last was made in 1963.

The only special-bodied TR to go into production in Great Britain was the Dové GTR4 based, as its name would suggest, on the TR4. This was identical with a TR4 back to the screen and below the waistline, but had a full-length and rather angular fixed-head roof, which did the same job as the MGB GT (and pre-dated it by two years). The rear window opened upwards and doubled as a loading hatch.

The conversion was built by Thomas Harringtons of Worthing (who also made the attractive Sunbeam Harrington Alpines) and was marketed by L.F. Dove Ltd, of Wimbledon, who were Triumph dealers. The major mechanical change was that a 15-gallon fuel tank was fitted under the boot floor with a filler cap in the vertical restyled panel below the opening rear hatch. In place of the standard fuel tank was a full-width occasional seat suitable for two children, the back rest of which could be folded forward to give a 40-inch-long load floor.

The Dové's problem was that it was both heavy (2,660lb as tested by *Autocar* in 1963) and expensive; at a time when a hardtop TR4 cost £949, the GTR4 sold for £1,250, and both acceleration and fuel consumption were adversely affected by the additional weight. The GTR4 was on the market from the spring of 1963 until the end of the TR4's run at the beginning of 1965, but was never offered on the basis of the TR4A.

CHAPTER 8

Buying an older TR

What to look for, restoration and the 'Best Buys'

It is much easier to write this chapter on TRs than it would be, for example, if I was talking about Jaguar E Types or vintage Bentleys. At least there are many thousands of TRs on the market in reasonably good condition, and there isn't an insane cult surrounding them which has boosted their price beyond all reasonable reach.

Even so, I am on a hiding to nothing as any recommendations I make will reflect my own personal preferences. There is, after all, much to be said for buying an early TR2 just *because* it is an early one and the design was the original. On the other hand, the fastest of all the TRs were the early TR5s . . . but wouldn't a 1969-70 TR6 with the same engine tune be preferable . . . and aren't there people who want the 'classic' mechanicals in the later chassis and body, which means that they like a TR4A . . . . and wait — how many people who talk so much about the TR7 have actually driven one yet? The secondhand TR7 market is already filling up nicely.

You see what I mean? So all I can do is point out some of the joys and pitfalls of TR-hunting, and without (I hope) giving offence to existing owners I can point out the minor failings now known on each model. But there is an invisible yet almost tangible barrier between the TR enthuisast who would never buy anything built with a Michelotti or a Karmann body, and the TR enthusiast who wants his pleasure in comfort and warmth and to whom the basic rigours of motoring in a TR3A make no sense at all.

Choosing, buying and running an older TR must inevitably be influenced by considerations of spares, service and maintenance. This is discussed in more detail in the next chapter, but basically

I recommend that nobody buys a 'classic' four-cylinder TR if he expects it to be maintained by a Triumph dealership. The garages are very busy, but thoroughly used to dealing with TR7s, and probably with the six-cylinder TR6s. Mechanically, therefore, they should be able to cope with the TR5s as well, but before that — forget it. Even the last of the TR4s, after all, is ten years old, and it is asking a lot for a garage to be actively interested in models of that age.

So which TR is for you? A rhetorical question which needs several others to follow it? Do you want mechanical simplicity or sophistication? Outright performance or reliability? Noise or refinement? Are you a spartan or a sybarite? There is — you see — a TR for most of you.

Basically, a 'classic' TR (TR2/TR3/TR3A/TR3B) was simple, reliable, quick enough, but not very refined. Comfort and warmth came after function — a formula which succeeded remarkably well for nearly ten years.

The TR4s and TR4As were true 'interim' cars. Most of the older TR simplicity was retained, but the creature comforts were greatly improved. A hardtop version could be very snug and very civilized. I can even split these models into two — the TR4 with its TR3A-type chassis was almost as easy to maintain as the 'classic' TRs, while the TR4A got the more complex chassis and usually the independent rear suspension of the later cars.

The TR5s and TR6s were considerably more complex and more refined than any previous TRs. Even though the Press were happy to look fondly on a TR6 and talk about it as 'the last of the hairy-chested sports cars', it was still a far cry from the rugged machines of the 1950s. The chassis — and the rear suspension in particular — was not something which could cheerfully be neglected, while the engines were really rather complicated.

Not that the basic layout of the 2,498cc 'six' was complex or even sophisticated, but the 'federal' carburation and anti-emission gear on one version of the car, and the expensive Lucas fuel injection on the other version, both made it a forbidding unit to face the amateur mechanic.

Let me first look at the choice of 'classic' TRs. Although well over 80,000 of all types were built between August 1953 and October 1962, a good many have disappeared, and of course the vast majority were exported. The TR2 was always relatively rare — only 8,628 were built in 27 months — and a good many of those remaining have been up-dated to look like TR3As. The TR3A was by far the most numerous of all — 58,236 built from September 1957 to October 1961 — and is the variant most people prefer. But why?

Triumph have very little of which to be ashamed — each of the 'classic' TRs was an improvement over the last. The TR3 had more engine power and better equipment than the TR2, the later TR3s had disc brakes (a world 'first' in this category and class), while the TR3As had both better equipment and the option of a more powerful 2,138cc engine.

Most TR enthusiasts agree that the first few TR2s might be rather sweet, and probably very economical, but they were in so many ways rather non-standard compared with later cars. It was not so much the important items — the 'long' doors and the original-specification Lockheed brakes are good examples — but the minor ones like the thermostat/radiator arrangement, the hastily-tooled body items (the first few hundred cars, for instance, had aluminium bonnet pressings), and the lack of extras which became available later.

The question of extras is something which makes the search for an outstanding TR so interesting. Some of those early cars will have been treated to later options of course. However, it is as well to point out that although the showroom price of a TR in the 1950s was always for the basic model, many cars were delivered dripping with all manner of very functional extras.

If I were looking for a 'classic' TR it would certainly have to have disc brakes (I wouldn't even settle for a 1955-56 model with the all-round 10in Lockheed drums), but it would also have to have wire wheels, radial-ply tyres, a steel hardtop and an overdrive. I'm not at all sure I would need the 'occasional' (very occasional!) seat, but it would be nice to find the hardtop car also equipped with the makings of a soft-top hood and sticks, and I would certainly insist on the optional heater, even if it was of the rather feeble recirculating variety.

The radial-ply tyres, of course, would have been fitted fairly recently (and a TR handles much better on modern radials than it ever did on cross-plies or steel-braced Michelin Xs), but everything else could be a factory-fitted option. I wouldn't object to a glass-fibre hardtop instead of the pressed-steel item (pre-1956 models), but I would want to be sure of an overdrive working on top, third and second gears (post-TS6266) and would prefer a TR3A with a post-TS60001 retooled body-shell.

For road use there are very few so-called 'competition' accessories which are essential. You certainly do not need a sump shield, or an oil cooler, but a couple of extra driving lamps make a difference to night driving, and the very latest in headlamp equipment never goes amiss.

I would not wish to own one of the very early TR2s with its dreadfully noisy exhaust system (but surely all of these mercifully have corroded away by now?), and I would hope that the later type of sliding sidescreens would have been added by now.

Lastly, of course, wouldn't it be nice to have the even lustier optional 2,138cc engine? Incidentally, you have no way of telling a 2,138cc from a 1,991cc engine at a casual glance. Only a strip-out and a cylinder-bore measurement will confirm this. Remember, too, that conversion to the 86mm cylinder bores is done very simply — and many TRs have been uprated in this way over the years. It doesn't harm the reliability one bit, and does great things for the pulling power.

Most of the above remarks still apply to the interim TR4s and TR4As. Overdrive, wire wheels and a hardtop were all optional, and some of the TR4s were fitted with the smaller 1,991cc engine. Most TR experts agree that a TR4 should have the later reshaped seats, but that it should also have SU carburettors. The early Strombergs were a bit too new to perform absolutely flawlessly and they gave rather more trouble in service (measured principally by guarantee claims), which explains why the specification changed several times in the mid-1960's.

Heaters were still optional, but most cars seem to have them, and as they are a much more efficient fresh-air design I would want one in my car. The face-level ventilation is a boon and a great advance on anything MG or Austin-Healey could provide for years. Quite a few TR4s had brake servos, and on the TR4A it was an official factory-fitted extra.

TR enthusiasts argue at length about rear suspensions. The live-axle cars had suffered from a lack of wheel movement (particularly on rebound) which made a TR's handling limits both well-known and carefully respected. The independently-suspended TR4A chassis (North American owners of live-axle TR4As must bear with me) was a great advance *if* the splined drive-shafts continued to behave themselves. The problem, also found on the Triumph 2000 saloons and the Stag, was that there was a tendency for the splines to stick when under full power if they were not perfectly lubricated. This was all very well in a straight line, but if this happened during cornering the suspension movement was effectively arrested and the cars tended to lift their inside rear wheel — or disengage the 'lock' with a jerk.

It is important that the rubber boots surrounding these splines, which are part way along the exposed drive-shafts, should be intact, that there should be no road filth attacking the splines, and that they should be well-lubricated.

In regard to the body, there is no doubt that the hardtop, with its cast rear window surround, is heavy, but it should also be very wind- and weather-proof. The optional 'Surrey-top' is not as common as many would hope; a TR with the top panel of its hardtop removed gives excellent 'Targa' motoring on a fine day. Incidentally, Porsche re-invented this later, and let everybody think it was their own idea!

You will want a six-cylinder TR if you want performance and refinement, but don't expect it to be simple to maintain. The fuel-injected 2,498cc engine was dropped from the Triumph 2.5 saloon range in 1975 because of systems problems and unnecessary complications, and if the TR6 had carried on for longer than it did I suspect it would have come in for the same treatment.

Treat the metering unit on the injection engine as a 'black box' which is not to be probed, and hope against hope that you won't have trouble with it — if you do you will have to buy a complete new one, and they are expensive.

Most of us think the factory over-reacted to criticism of low-speed problems with the original highly-tuned TR5/TR6 models because of their ambitious camshaft timing. Certainly the 1973 and later TR6s were considerably slower than the original models, even if they did give a smoother idle condition and less temperament. Any TR6 customer with red blood in his veins will be looking for a pre-1973 model, or at least a more recent example (complete with chin spoiler and decoration) in which the engine has been reconverted to the original tune; quite a number have.

I also prefer pre-1973 models for their lusty old overdrive — and particularly for the overdrive second which went with it — and for their less obvious decoration and badging. Whether you like a Michelotti TR5 or a Karmann TR6 is a matter of choice, and I will have nothing to do with giving my opinion, other than to say that I prefer the old-style hardtop which was optional on the TR5.

Carburetted TR6s, all sold in the United States where a TR enthusiast never had the choice of fuel-injected performance, all perform in much the same way, and anyone who feels like trying to maintain those complex de-toxed engines has my admiration and blessing! My only comment is that each year the necessary hang-on equipment proliferated, the extra 'safety' items sprouted, the weight increased and the petrol tank capacity progressively shrank. Assuming that you are not a safety 'nut' — and most North American motorists are not — you should look around for an elderly TR6, which will offend you least!

As I have already mentioned in an earlier chapter, wire wheels were withdrawn from the TR6 options list in 1973, and the optional J-Type overdrive was standardized from the start of 1974 model-year machines. The later (mid-1971 and afterwards) models had stronger but slighter wider-ratio gearboxes than had the TR5s and early TR6s. There is a body of opinion which says that the ideal set-up, therefore, was supplied between mid-1971 and the end of 1972, when this box was combined with the older 'A'-Type overdrive.

There is very little to say about TR7s at this stage, as the range and its variations are still building up. However, it is the only TR on which you can buy automatic transmission (the well-proven Borg-Warner three-speed Type 65), and while there is no overdrive option at least there is a five-speed gearbox instead.

Five-speed TR7s are rare in Britain and increasingly common in the United States (this market having been given priority). I certainly like the five-speed gearbox very much; it seems to be virtually bomb-proof, and it has the added advantage of being sold along with the medium-duty axle, the bigger rear brakes and the fatter low-profile tyres.

If you dearly want a 16-valve TR7 you'll either have to wait for the forthcoming production model to be announced, convert the engine yourself, or have it done by the TR specialists who have already spied a market for this sort of work. My own view is that it is more important to raise a four-speed TR7's gearing than its performance. The basic model is undergeared, in spite of what the factory might protest. This remark applies to non-'federal' models which rev more freely and produce more power; 'federal' cars are suitably de-toxed and are not nearly as fast. The only answer is to look for a higher ratio than the 3.63:1 which is standard; a GT6's 3.27:1 would fit, but that would probably make the car too high-geared. There doesn't seem to be a happy medium as the 3.45:1 ratio from the old TR6 will not fit at any price — the crownwheel-and-pinion sets and the differentials which go with them are entirely different designs.

There isn't a lot I need to say on the question of restoration of recent TRs; it doesn't apply to TR7s, and hopefully not yet to TR6s. As far as the older models are concerned, restoration is more concerned with the availability and authenticity of spare parts rather than whether a TR is worth restoring at all. I deal with spare parts in Chapter 9, and I can vouch for the fact that almost *any* TR can be restored, assuming that its chassis is in an uncrashed condition.

The chassis are robust and, like most other separate frames which were properly designed in the first place, they resist corrosion for many years. Broadly speaking, if an old and seemingly derelict TR has a good chassis, is mechanically complete, and is of a variant for which spare parts can be obtained from one source or another, then it can be and is worth being restored.

Most of the deterioration takes place in the sheet metal of the body-shell. Fortunately, because this adds little strength to the chassis of a TR, this means that a scruffy TR can survive for years, getting more and more tatty, without the car's integrity being threatened. The TR clubs can advise on the tell-tale points to investigate, but basically it is the body parts exposed to road filth — wings, wheel-arches and particularly the floors and boot floors — which suffer most. A badly corroded TR floor is something about which to be horrified. This means either a monster rebuild (expensive), a new body-shell transplant (difficult as supplies are virtually unavailable for old models), or a bodge-up job (not recommended and very undesirable).

The engines and transmissions, as must have become clear in this book, have an enviable reputation. A four-cylinder engine rebuild rarely involves more than new liners, piston rings, bearings and attention to the valve gear. An engine which breaks (literally breaks vital rotating parts) is almost unknown, unless it has been brutally misused for many thousands of miles. Gearboxes are strong, simple and easily rebuilt. One member of the British TR Register (Pete Cox) makes quite a business out of this, and needs only the simplest of equipment. Axles — live or independent — all have very strong differentials and gears, except that the early TR2s had rather suspect mounting bolts in the differential, and the TR2 half-shafts are known to snap if thoroughly abused (whereas later live-axle shafts, in axles of the Vanguard type, are more nearly idiot-proof).

Brakes, suspensions, steering and other chassis items are all, in the main, simple, strong and reliable. Along with the other chassis features, this makes it almost a pleasure (if a lengthy and none-too-cheap one) to undertake a complete TR rebuild.

The word which keeps recurring in this section is 'simple', coupled with 'reliable'. Isn't that what most of the charm of a TR is all about?

CHAPTER 9

Spares and maintenance

Factory, TR Register and VTR facilities

To use a well-hackneyed phrase, there is good news and bad news. The good news is that Triumph themselves hold spares for all TRs — even some parts for TR3s and TR2s. The bad news is that when the older items go out of stock the factory has no intention of replacing them. To a TR2 owner who desperately needs a few bits and pieces to restore his car this might sound callous. But surely the factory cannot be castigated for dropping support for cars built so long ago? Remember, *all* TR2s and TR3s are now at least 20 years old.

Fortunately that is not the end of the story. Because of the efforts of Triumph TR enthusiasts' clubs in Britain and in the United States, a worn-out TR doesn't have to be written-off. Sometimes in connivance with the factory, but often by their own persistence, these clubs manage to plug the gaps left by the empty bins in the factory or in concessionaires' service and spare parts buildings.

But don't get me wrong. When a model goes out of production Triumph does not abandon it to its fate. The fact that there was a sudden famine of TR6 body skin panels almost as soon as the car was dropped in 1976 was not intentional — merely that the factory were moving the tools from one plant to another, and negotiating new methods for filling up the spares pipeline. By the time this book is published that embarrassing hiccup should have been cured.

It is Triumph's (and therefore Leyland's) policy to support a car for at least ten years after it goes out of production, but we all know that this rule is not absolute Holy Writ. Many TR2/TR3 parts — almost all being mechanical items shared with cars like the Standard Vanguard — are still available from Coventry. On the other hand parts for the short-lived TR5/TR250 which are unique to this variant are, and always have been, in very short supply. Already some TR6 parts are becoming scarce.

Unhappily for TR enthusiasts, their cars are not supported in the same way as Rolls-Royce look after their obsolete models. Once a model is taken out of production an estimate, based on many years of practical experience, is made of the demand for any particular item, and a once-and-for-all run-out quantity is manufactured. That, usually, is that. In exceptional cases (and it's no good pleading with the factory that the part you need is an exceptional case) another batch of spares has been made, but in almost every instance the tools are then either put away, abandoned to the weather, or — worse — scrapped altogether.

The situation regarding paint is eased by the fact that the correct colours can always be synthesised by the experts in this sort of thing if the original 'mix' is known. One of the first categories of spares to go missing are trim items. The reason for this is clear — whereas one lamp or one gear wheel will suit any TR3A (say), there might be more than a dozen trim options, and Triumph do not find it profitable to keep a small stock of every door trim panel, every carpet, every seat, or every cover panel.

However (and this is where the specialist knowledge of the clubs comes in handy) some colours and trim materials were used for many years. If you can identify a material (and perhaps supply a tiny sample for comparison) you may well find that the factory has kept the material itself in stock. Making up the seats from sheets of vinyl or trim pads is your own affair . . . . . .

So this is where the clubs can be so useful. Not only do they *care* very deeply about the TRs, but they are developing a vitally important and excellently researched spares supply system. This probably sounds like a well-paid commercial for the one-make clubs, but I simply do not see how anyone can own an ageing 'classic' and hope to restore and maintain it properly without belonging to the appropriate club!

This is not, however, an indictment of the factory. It is really asking too much to expect a factory service or technical department to be very interested in products more than ten years obsolete. The designers and development engineers are already working on the TRs of the 1980s, and even the TR7s, in production since 1974 and cleared for production since 1973, are old hat to them. Already they will have passed off the more exciting TR7 variants which we know are coming, and possibly other major developments which we *hope* are coming. Some of them, the romantics, the more reminiscent, and the hoarders of information, may still know a lot about the TR6, but we can't expect them to have facts about the TR2/TR3/TR4 at their finger tips.

This is why the TR clubs are now very important. Not only do they cater for their members in supplying nostalgia and fellowship, but they are the source of expertise and detailed knowledge. Before going into detail with addresses and information I have to give a big 'Thank You' to the TR Register of Great Britain and their secretary, Alan Robinson, without whom this book would certainly have been less complete and accurate. (I hope to goodness that between us we haven't allowed any mistakes to slip through!)

In Britain, then, the important organization for any Triumph TR owner is the TR Register. If you are a member already I am preaching to the converted, but if not you should know this:

The club was founded in 1970 to 'preserve the marque TR2/TR3/TR3A', but by 1977 there were so many associate members with later TRs that its scope was widened to cover all the TR sports cars built before the TR7. Naturally it is very strong in Britain, but there are now branches in many parts of the world.

The TR Register's secretary is: Valerie Simpson,
The TR Register,
271 High Street,
Berkhamsted,
Herts HP4 1AA

Apart from the *Newsletter*, which is getting bigger and looking more professional every time I see it, there is a regular spares bulletin.

Two people — Pete Cox and Pete Buckles — dominate the TR spares business, in partnership but living 100 miles apart. Their addresses are as follows:

Pete Cox
Cox & Buckles Spares,
89 Fairfax Road,
West Heath,
Birmingham 31

Pete Buckles
Cox & Buckles Spares,
Market Road,
Richmond,
Surrey

Cox specializes in new spares, Buckles in both new and used spares. Another useful address for TR owners in the London area is The TR Shop Ltd, 16 Chiswick High Road, London W4.

The factory spares department makes the point that if they do not stock a spare part themselves, and it was originally made for them by a supplier, it is highly unlikely that the supplier will have any spares either. This does not apply to proprietary items (electrical distributors, coils and lamps are examples), but where something like a road spring, a suspension damper, or steering parts were especially manufactured for the factory.

Cox and Buckles tackle this problem in two ways. They are continually on the look-out for windfall supplies of spare parts, which might come to them as a result of a Triumph dealership clearing out a corner of his stores, or when a garage changes its franchises. Things continue to appear, and it is really quite amazing where certain hard-to-find spares can be found.

Their second method is more complex, more enterprising, and altogether more expensive to organize. It is, quite simply, to trace back a part to its original-equipment supplier and see if new parts can be manufactured. The last time I talked to Pete Buckles he pointed out that a supplier often keeps his tools much longer than a big factory would, and he showed me various body and body fitting parts which had just been manufactured for obsolete TRs on the original tools and to original specifications. This sort of thing becomes problematical when major items are involved, but at the last count I know that arrangements were in hand to have supplies of TR2/3/3A/3B wings manufactured.

The TR Register, too, has a technical editor, whose job (unpaid, of course) is to co-ordinate all the restoration/ maintenance/service information for the benefit of members.

In particular, the Register's knowledge now covers the interchangeability of nominally non-TR mechanical items which are nevertheless perfectly usable in a TR. In many cases the parts are virtually the same, and built to equally exacting specifications, but are given different Triumph Part Numbers! Once bitten with the TR bug, and having learned how much cross-fertilization there always was with other Standard-Triumph products, you will realize that components from the Standard Vanguard, the Ensign, and even the Triumph 2000/2.5PI might all be interchangeable with a TR's parts.

With this in mind, the Register recently published an invaluable booklet, called *Technicalities — Volume One* (price £2.00 to Register members), which is basically a collection of edited articles first published in the *Newsletter*. From this you can learn which axle ratios and which gear clusters give which effect, which brakes match which suspensions, and which bodies go with which mechanicals. It concentrates on the 'classic' TRs from 1953 to 1962, but I have no doubt that later-model owners would also benefit.

In North America where, after all, the majority of all TRs have been sold, TR interests are looked after by the Vintage Triumph Register. As the title of the club suggests, it caters for all Triumphs ever made — saloon or sporting, pre-war or post-war, new and not-so-new, but as one might expect the lion's share of membership, of interest, and of coverage is given over to TRs.

First, the addresses:
Membership Secretary: Terry Telke,
10815 Russell Avenue South,
Bloomington,
Minnesota 55431

President: Randy Mason,
23060 Beech Street,
Dearborn,
Michigan 48124

The VTR (as it is always known) aims to do the same for North American TR owners as the TR Register does for those in Britain. There are several active branches of the VTR in Canada, and separate 'chapters' are dotted all over the United States which — need I remind anyone — is a mighty big place.

In North America, of course, Triumph are centred on Leonia,

New Jersey. As it just so happens that Michael Cook, their Public Relations Manager, is also an old-car nut and a member of VTR, too, it is easy to see that the club and the factory are quite close together. In the United States, the same situation applies over spares and spare-parts stocking, though as there are many more TRs in existence there, the chances of finding spares for old models are proportionately higher. Like the TR Register, VTR is looking for ways to manufacture new spares which are otherwise obsolete, but at the moment they are leaning heavily on the TR Register for expertise and supplies.

Even so, these names are important:

Spares Chairman:	TR Spare Parts Service:
Bill Redinger,	John Manning,
44571 Westminster Way,	Box 126,
Plymouth,	Flourtown,
Michigan 48170	Pennsylvania 19131

The VTR, too, is distinguished by having a really first-class bi-monthly magazine — *The Vintage Triumph* — edited by that distinguished young historian Richard Langworth.

Both clubs keep a library of publications important to the Triumph TR owner, including in many cases reprints of or references to original magazine road tests, and up-to-date lists of factory publications. Here are the factory publications still available at the time of writing (summer 1977):

		Part No.
Owners' handbooks:	TR4A	512916
	TR5	545034
	TR6	545078
	TR7 (UK etc)	RTC9210
	TR7 (USA 'federal')	RTC9209/77

(No handbooks for TR2 to TR4 models remain in stock.)

		Part No.
Repair operation manuals:	TR5	545053
	(Supplement to TR4 manual no longer available)	
	TR4/4A/5/250/6	AKM3646 **
	TR7-1976 model	RTC9200
	TR7-1977 model	AKM3079

**This is a brand-new publication which brings together all the necessary information about what I would call the Michelotti/Karmann-bodied TRs, starting from the TR4 of 1961 and running through to the TR6. I found it fascinating because of the way it grouped together the technical specification summaries, and made it easy to understand how one model evolved into the other, and — in the case of 'federal' models — how the tune and specification changed slightly from year to year.

Spare parts catalogues:

	Part No.
TR4	510978
TR4A	514837
TR5/TR250	516915
TR6	517785A
TR7	RTC9020A

The Part No of the TR2/3/3A spare parts catalogue was 501293, but these are now out of print, and a copy is something of a collector's item among TR enthusiasts. Apparently Triumph have no plans to reprint it.

Triumph acknowledge the spare-parts problem where old TRs are concerned, and recommend the following course of action:

(a) First try to establish the actual part number of the component you need; nobody, not even a TR historic enthusiast, likes being asked for a rear suspension thingummy for an-er-I think TR3 — but it could be a TR2 . . . . .

(b) Armed with this number, see if your Triumph dealer can supply, or knows if the part is available. Is he a bit reluctant to ask? Then persist. Triumph point out that although they have a Customer Relations Department, who can advise on parts availability, they cannot supply parts direct to a private customer. So whatever your difficulties in gaining the sympathies of the spare parts manager at your local dealership, you must order all factory-held spares through him.

(c) Be a member of the TR Register or the VTR, and get your parts through their organization instead.

Incidentally, most TR owners know that glass-fibre body skin panels can be purchased to make good a rusty body-shell. These, while light in weight and guaranteed to be rust-free in the future, have snags. In some cases they don't seem to fit very well, while the question of originality is important. Among true TR enthusiasts, a car with glass-fibre parts is looked down-upon, and there is no doubt that its eventual resale value will be somewhat lower than if genuine steel wings or bonnet panels are used.

In the end, however, it is the driving and the enjoyment of your TR which is most important. Happily, a TR has a phenomenal reputation for reliability, for guts and for sheer long life. That is why so many of them, well past their first flush of youth, are still in daily use. They gave great pleasure when new, and continue to do so. A sports car really doesn't need any better summing-up than that.

A new shape on the SCCA racing scene; the TR7 convertible became a production car class winner in its major export market.

The end?
Let us hope not!

APPENDIX A

Technical specifications

20TS prototype (later dubbed TR1) — 1952 model
Engine: 4-cyl, 83 × 92mm, 1,991cc, CR 7.0:1, 2 SU carbs. 75bhp (net) at 4,500rpm. Maximum torque 105lb ft at 2,300rpm.
Transmission: Axle ratio 3.89:1. Overall gear ratios 3.89, 5.15, 7.81, 13.15, reverse 16.66:1. 19.0mph/1,000rpm in top gear.
Suspension and brakes: Ifs, coil springs, wishbones and telescopic dampers; live rear axle, half-elliptic leaf springs, lever-arm dampers. Cam-and-lever steering. 9 × 1¾in front and rear drum brakes. 5.50-15in tyres on 4.0in rims.
Dimensions: Wheelbase 7ft 4in; front track 3ft 9in; rear track 3ft 9.5in; length 11ft 9in; width 4ft 7.5in; height (hood up) 4ft 3in. Unladen weight 1,708lb.
Basic price: £555. Only one prototype built.

TR2 — produced 1953 to 1955
Engine: 4-cyl, 83 × 92mm, 1,991cc, CR 8.5:1, 2 SU carbs. 90bhp (gross) at 4,800rpm. Maximum torque 117lb ft at 3,000rpm.
Transmission: Axle ratio 3.7:1. Overall gear ratios 3.7, 4.90, 7.43, 12.51, reverse 16.09:1. Optional overdrive, ratio 3.03:1. 20mph/1,000rpm in direct top gear, 24.5mph/1,000rpm in overdrive.
Suspension and brakes: Ifs, coil springs, wishbones and telescopic dampers; live rear axle, half-elliptic leaf springs, lever-arm dampers. Cam-and-lever steering. 10 × 2¼in front brakes, 9 × 1¾in rear brakes (from autumn 1954 10 × 2¼in brakes all round). 5.50-15in tyres on 4.0in rims (later 4.5in rims).
Dimensions: Wheelbase 7ft 4in; front track 3ft 9in; rear track 3ft 9.5in; length 12ft 7in; width 4ft 7.5in; height (hood up) 4ft 2in. Unladen weight 1,848lb.
Basic price: £555 at first, £595 from January 1954, £625 from October 1954.

TR3 — produced 1955 to 1957
Specification as for TR2 except for:
Engine: 95bhp at 4,800rpm, later 100bhp at 5,000rpm.
Brakes (from Chassis No TS13046, October 1956): 11in front discs, 10 × 2¼in rear drums.
Unladen weight 1,988lb.
Basic price: £650 at first, £680 from May 1956.

TR3A — produced 1957 to 1961
Specification as for disc-braked TR3 except for:
Rear drum brakes (from Chassis No TS56377, autumn 1959): 9 × 1¾in.
Unladen weight 2,050lb.
Note: From 1959, there was an optional engine: 86 × 92mm, 2,138cc, CR 9.1:1. No official power or torque figures were ever released.
Basic price: £699 — unaltered for four years.

TR3B — produced 1962 (USA market only)
There were two series. Cars in TSF series had late-model 1,991cc TR3A engines; Cars in TCF series had early TR4 2,138cc engines. Both cars with all-synchromesh TR4 gearboxes. Overall gear ratios 3.7, 4.90, 7.43, 11.61, reverse 11.92:1; synchromesh on all forward gears. Optional overdrive, 20mph/1,000rpm in direct top gear, 24.4mph/1,000rpm in overdrive.
Basic price: These cars were never sold in Great Britain.

TR4 — produced 1961 to 1965
Engine: 4-cyl, 86 × 92mm, 2,138cc, CR 9.0:1, 2 SU carbs (or 2 Stromberg carbs). 100bhp (net) at 4,600rpm. Maximum torque 127lb ft at 3,350rpm. Optional 2-litre TR3A engine.
Transmission: Axle ratio 3.7:1. Overall gear ratios 3.7, 4.90, 7.43, 11.61, reverse 11.92:1. Synchromesh on all forward gears. Optional overdrive 3.32:1 (with 4.1:1 axle ratio). 20mph/1,000rpm in direct top gear, 22.2mph/1,000rpm in overdrive.
Suspension and brakes: Ifs, coil springs, wishbones and telescopic dampers; live rear axle, half-elliptic leaf springs, lever-arm dampers. Rack-and-pinion steering. 11in diameter front disc brakes, 9 × 1¾in rear drums. 5.90-15in tyres.
Dimensions: Wheelbase 7ft 4in; front track 4ft 1in; rear track 4ft 0in; length 12ft 9.6in; width 4ft 9.5in; height (hood up) 4ft 2in. Unladen weight 2,128lb.
Basic price: £750.

TR4A — produced 1965 to 1967

Specification as for late-model TR4 except for: Engine: 104bhp (net) at 4,700rpm. Maximum torque 132lb ft at 3,000rpm. No 2-litre engine option. Rear suspension: Irs, coil springs, semi-trailing arms, lever-arm dampers. Optional (USA market only) live axle, half-elliptic leaf springs and lever-arm dampers. 6.95-15in tyres.
Rear track 4ft 0.5in. Unladen weight 2,240lb.
Basic price: £800.

TR5 — produced 1967 and 1968

Engine: 6-cyl, 74.7 × 95mm, 2,498cc, CR 9.5:1, Lucas indirect fuel injection. 150bhp (net) at 5,500rpm. Maximum torque 164lb ft at 3,500rpm.
Transmission: Axle ratio 3.45:1. Overall gear ratios 3.45, 4.59, 6.92, 10.80, reverse 11.11:1. Optional overdrive 2.82:1. 21.2mph/1,000rpm in direct top gear, 25.9mph/1,000rpm in overdrive.
Suspension and brakes: Ifs, coil springs, wishbones and telescopic dampers; irs, coil springs, semi-trailing arms, lever-arm dampers. Rack-and-pinion steering. 10.9in front disc brakes, 9 × 1¾in rear drums, and vacuum-servo assistance. 165-15in radial-ply tyres on 5.0in rims.
Dimensions: Wheelbase 7ft 4in; front track 4ft 1.25in; rear track 4ft 0.75in; length 12ft 9.6in; width 4ft 10in; height 4ft 2in. Unladen weight 2,268lb.
Basic price: £985.

TR250 — produced 1967 and 1968 (USA market only)

Specification as for TR5 except for:
Engine: CR 8.5:1, 2 Stromberg carburettors. 104bhp (net) at 4,500rpm. Maximum torque 143lb ft at 3,000rpm. Axle ratio 3.7:1. Overall gear ratios 3.7, 4.90, 7.43, 11.61, reverse 11.92:1. Optional A-Type overdrive, 3.03:1. 20.75mph/1,000rpm in direct top gear, 25.3mph/1,000rpm in overdrive. 185SR-15in radial-ply tyres.

TR6 (Non-USA versions) — produced 1969 to 1975

Basic specification as for TR5 except for:
Engine: 1969-72 models had TR5 engine specification. From start of CR-series Commission Numbers engine power was reduced and recalibrated to 124bhp (DIN) at 5,000rpm. Maximum torque became 143lb ft at 3,500rpm.
Transmission: TR5 ratios until mid-1971.
From gearbox numbers CD51163/CC89817, revised internal ratios gave overall gearing of 3.45, 4.78, 7.25, 10.33, reverse 11.62:1.
From 1973 model (Commission Number CR567 onward) J-Type overdrive replaced A-Type overdrive. Overall ratio 2.75:1 26.6mph/1,000rpm in overdrive.
Suspension: Anti-roll bar added to front suspension and 5.5in wheel rims in place of 5.0in rims.
Dimensions: Length 13ft 3in; width 4ft 10in. Unladen weight 2,473lb.
Basic price £1,020 on 1969 announcement, £1,045 in January 1970, £1,111 in January 1971, £1,220 in January 1972, £1,340 in January 1973, then raised by leaps and bounds to £2,022 when the TR7 was announced in January 1975, and finally to £2,335 when discontinued officially in the autumn of 1975.

TR6 (USA 'federal' version) — produced 1969 to 1976

Basic specification as for TR5, except for:
Engine (1969-71): CR 8.5:1, 2 Stromberg carburettors. 104bhp (net) at 4,500rpm. Maximum torque 143lb ft at 3,000rpm.
(1972-73): CR 7.75:1, 2 Stromberg carburettors. 106bhp (net) at 4,900rpm. Maximum torque 133lb ft at 3,000rpm.
(1974-76): CR 7.5:1, 2 Stromberg carburettors. 106bhp (net) at 4,900rpm. Maximum torque 133lb ft at 3,000rpm.
Transmission: Axle ratio 3.7:1. Overall gear ratios 3.7, 4.90, 7.43, 11.61, reverse 11.92:1. Optional overdrive 3.03:1. 20.75mph/1,000rpm in direct top gear, 25.3mph/1,000rpm in overdrive.
From gearbox numbers CD51163/CC89817 (introduced mid-1971) revised internal gear ratios gave overall gearing of 3.7, 5.14, 7.77, 11.06, reverse 12.47:1.
From 1973 model (Commission Numbers CF1 onwards and CR567 onwards) J-Type overdrive replaced A-Type overdrive. Overall ratio 2.95:1. 26.1mph/1,000rpm in overdrive.
Suspension: Anti-roll bar added to front suspension and 5.5in wheel rims in place of 5.0in rims.
Dimensions: Length 13ft 3in (1969-72), 13ft 6.1in (1973-74), 13ft 7.6in (1975-76). Unladen weight 2,390lb (1969-74), 2,438lb (1975-76).
Basic price: These cars were never sold in Great Britain.

TR7 (USA 'federal' version) — introduced in January 1975

Engine: 4-cyl, single-overhead-camshaft, 90.3 × 78mm, 1,998cc, CR 8.0:1, 2 Stromberg carbs. Approximately 92bhp (DIN) at 5,000rpm. Maximum torque approximately 115lb ft at 3,500rpm.
Transmission: Axle ratio 3.63:1. Overall gear ratios 3.63, 4.56, 6.47, 9.65, reverse 10.95:1. Overdrive not available. 17.9mph/1,000rpm in top gear. Optional: Borg-Warner Type 65 automatic transmission. Axle ratio 3.27:1. Overall ratios 3.27, 4.74, 7.82, reverse 6.83:1. 19.9mph/1,000rpm in direct drive. Optional: (1976-77) 5-speed manual gearbox. Axle ratio 3.9:1. Overall gear ratios 3.25, 3.90, 5.44, 8.14, 12.95, reverse 13.37:1. 20.8mph/1,000rpm in fifth gear.
Suspension and brakes: Ifs, coil springs, MacPherson struts, anti-roll bar; rear, live axle, coil springs, radius arms, anti-roll bar and telescopic dampers. Rack-and-pinion steering. 9.7in front discs, 8 × 1.5in rear drums and vacuum-servo assistance. 9 × 1.75in rear brakes with optional 5-speed gearbox. 185/70—13in or 175—13in radial-ply tyres.
Dimensions: Wheelbase 7ft 1in; front track 4ft 7.5in; rear track 4ft 7.3in; length 13ft 8.5in; width 5ft 6.2in; height 4ft 1.9in. Unladen weight 2,241lb, with 5-speed gearbox equipment 2,355lb.
Basic price: Not available in Great Britain.
Note: For the 1981 model year, all cars were equipped with Bosch fuel injection. Manual transmission cars, axle ratio 3.45:1. Overall gear ratios 2.74, 3.45, 4.83, 7.21, 11.45:1; reverse 11.83:1. 24.7mph/1,000rpm in fifth gear. Automatic transmission cars, axle ratio 3.08:1. Overall gear ratios 3.08, 4.47, 7.36:1, reverse 6.44:1. 22.0mph/1,000rpm in top gear. 8in rear brakes

no longer fitted — 9in brakes standard. 175—13in tyres no longer fitted, 185/70—13in tyres standard. Convertible 32lb heavier than coupe.

TR7 (Non-USA version) — introduced May 1976

Basic specification as for USA 'federal' version of TR7 except for:

Engine: CR 9.25:1; 2 SU carbs. 105bhp (DIN) at 5,500rpm. Maximum torque 119lb ft at 3,500rpm.

Dimensions: Length 13ft 4.1in. Unladen weight 2,205lb, with 5-speed gearbox equipment 2,311lb.

Basic price: £2,564 when introduced in May 1976, £2,850 in January 1977, £2,881 in May 1977.

Note: Convertible body style introduced March 1980, weighing 2,356lb, compared with 2,324lb for 1980 TR7 Coupe. Gearing of pre-1981 'federal' TR7s retained for non-USA models for 1981.

Basic price: TR7 Convertible: £4,783 when introduced in March 1980, £5,045 in January 1981. TR7 Coupe: £5,229 in January 1981.

TR8 (USA 'federal' version) — introduced in Spring 1980, only with Convertible bodywork)

Basic specification as for four-cylinder TR7, except for:

Engine: V8-cyl, 88.9 × 71.1mm, 3,528cc, CR 8.1:1, 2 Stromberg carbs (Lucas fuel injection for California). 133bhp (DIN) on carbs, 137bhp (DIN) on injection, at 5,000rpm. Maximum torque (carbs) 174lb ft at 3,000rpm, (injection) 168lb ft at 3,250rpm.

Transmission: Axle ratio 3.08:1. Overall gear ratios 2.56, 3.08, 4.31, 6.44, 10.23:1, reverse 10.56:1. 26.1mph/1,000rpm in fifth gear. Optional: Borg-Warner Type 65 automatic transmission. Axle ratio 3.08:1. Overall gear ratios 3.08, 4.47, 7.36:1, reverse 6.44:1. 21.9mph/1,000rpm in top gear.

Suspension and brakes: 9 × 1.75in rear drums as standard. 185/70—13in tyres. Power-assisted steering.

Dimensions: Unladen weight 2,565lb.

Basic price: Not available in Great Britain.

Note: For 1981 model year, Lucas petrol injection was standardized on all USA-market cars and fifth gear was raised to 2.44:1, with 27.6mph/1,000rpm in fifth gear.

Commission Number sequences — model by model

Model	Years built	Variant	Commission No.
TR2	Aug 1953-Oct 1955	—	TS1-TS8636
TR3	Oct 1955-Sep 1956	With drum brakes	TS8637-TS13045
TR3	Sep 1956-Sep 1957	With disc brakes	TS13046-TS22013
TR3A	Sep 1957-Oct 1961		TS22014-TS82346
TR3B	Mar 1962-Sep 1962	Exactly as TR3A	TSF1-TSF530
TR3B	May 1962-Oct 1962	With TR4 engine and all-synchro box	TCF1-TCF2804
TR4	Aug 1961-Jan 1965	2-litre or 2.2-litre	CT1-CT40304
TR4A	Jan 1965-Aug 1967	With irs	CTC50001-CTC78684
	(with live axle prefix was CT . . . .)		
TR5	Oct 1967-Nov 1968	With fuel injection	CP1-CP3096
TR250	Aug 1967-Dec 1968	With carburettors	CD1-CD8594

Model	Years built	Variant	Commission No.
TR6	Nov 1968-Nov 1969	With fuel injection	CP25001-last figure not known
	Nov 1969-Nov 1972	With fuel injection	CP50001-CP77716
	Nov 1972-Jul 1975	With fuel injection	CR1-CR6701
TR6	Jan 1969-Nov 1969	'Federal' version with carburettors	CC25001-last figure not known
	Nov 1969-Sep 1972	''	CC50001-CC85737
	Sep 1972-Aug 1973	''	CF1-CF12500
	Aug 1973-Feb 1975	''	CF12501-CF35000
	Feb 1975-Jul 1976	''	CF35001-CF58328
TR7	Sep 1974 on	'Federal' version	ACL1 onwards
TR7	Sep 1975 on	Other markets	ACG1 onwards
		Other markets with five-speed box	ACG35F and later ACG . . . . F
	May 1978	Last car built at Speke, Liverpool	ACG 44328
	Oct 1978	First car built at Coventry	TCG 100000
TR8	Autumn 1979 on	'Federal' convertibles only	

TR deliveries — 1953 to date

The unique and detailed charts which follow show — year on year, model by model, home and export — the way in which Triumph TR sports cars have sold since 1953.

There are some discrepancies between the numbers of cars actually built and the quantities which could be inferred from a study of Commission Number sequences. This is explained by the existence of gaps in the numbering sequence, for which Triumph have given no explanation. Certain numbers, therefore, were never issued.

The charts, therefore, give the official Leyland Cars/Triumph statistics for all TRs. I should emphasize that these denote *deliveries* in any calendar year, which explains, for instance, why some TR4A sales occur in 1968 and a few TR6 sales in 1977.

The two really interesting aspects, never before detailed, are that 3,331 of the vary rare TR3Bs were built in 1962 (2,801 with the TR4 engine and all-synchromesh gearbox), and that in Triumph's crisis-torn 1961 year there was a near-collapse of TR3A deliveries.

It is also clear that the TR3A was the most popular of all TRs (in terms of sales in a given year) for a long period, until the TR7 finally got into its stride. The TR7 is already the most numerous of all TRs. The total of all TRs built is now fast approaching 400,000.

TOTAL DELIVERIES

Model	Years built	Home	Export	Total
TR2	Aug 1953-Oct 1955	2823	5805	8628
TR3	Oct 1955-Sep 1957	1286	12091	13377
TR3A	Sep 1957-Oct 1961	1896	56340	58236
TR3B	Mar 1962-Oct 1962	—	3331	3331
TR4	Aug 1961-Jan 1965	2592	37661	40253
TR4A	Jan 1965-Aug 1967	3075	25390	28465
TR5	Oct 1967-Nov 1968	1161	1786	2947
TR250	Aug 1967-Dec 1968	—	8484	8484
TR6	Nov 1968-Jul 1976	8370	86249	94619
TR7	Sept 1974 to end of 1980 only — production continues	23999	83719	107718
TR8	Autumn 1979 to end of 1980 only — production continues	68	2229	2297

Note: Figures for TR2, TR3, TR3A and TR3B differ slightly from those given in my book *The Story of Triumph Sports Cars.* This is due to separation of TR3B statistics and minor modifications on the part of the statistical department.

HOME MARKET DELIVERIES

Year	TR2	TR3	TR3A	TR4	TR4A	TR5 PI	TR6 PI	TR7 and TR8	Total for Year
1953	50								50
1954	1269								1269
1955	1504	226							1730
1956		613							613
1957		447							447
1958			542						542
1959			638						638
1960			640						640
1961			63	10					73
1962			13	964					977
1963				796					796
1964				819					819
1965				3	1073				1076
1966					1000				1000
1967					1002	25			1027
1968						1136			1136
1969							704		704
1970							1308		1308
1971							1288		1288
1972							1720		1720
1973							1948		1948
1974							843		843
1975							545	41*	
1976							14	6923*	
1977								8408*	
1978								1265*	
1979								2514*	
1980								4916*	

EXPORT MARKET DELIVERIES

Year	TR2	TR3	TR3A	TR3B	TR4	TR4A TR250	TR5	TR6 Carb	TR7 and TR8	Total for Year
1953	198									198
1954	3622									3622
1955	1985	684								2669
1956		4726								4726
1957		6681	3470							10151
1958			15454							15454
1959			20660							20660
1960			16414							16414
1961				342	2460					2802
1962				3326	14969					18295
1963				5	9286					9291
1964					10699					10699
1965					247	12662				12909
1966						10097				10097
1967						2619	2482			5101
1968						12	7788	1519		9319
1969								7981		7981
1970								10795		10795
1971								12203		12203
1972								11724		11724
1973								11705		11705
1974								13740		13740
1975								9228	15360*	
1976								7208	25820*	
1977								146	14528*	
1978									5517*	
1979									16348*	
1980									8375*	

Note: All TR7/TR8 statistics marked * denote *production* rather than actual *deliveries.* BL are no longer able to supply accurate delivery statistics.

Note: 1979 totals include 63 home market TR8 and 141 export TR8 models — all coupes, none of which were actually sold. 1980 totals include 5 home market TR8s and 2088 export TR8s, all convertibles.

APPENDIX D

How fast? How economical? How heavy?

I do not believe in quoting from factory handouts. The figures tabled here are those recorded by authoritative motoring magazines from test cars loaned to them by Triumph or by the North American subsidiary company. All except the last three are taken from *Autocar* tests; the last three are from tests published by the American publication *Road and Track.* I have not troubled to list *Road and Track* figures for models built before the TR250 as these were mechanically identical to home-market machines.

Neither *Autocar* nor *Motor* ever published a test of a TR3A, but this car could be expected to perform almost identically with a late-model TR3.

Incidentally, there is something very unlikely about the kerb weight of 2,464lb quoted by *Autocar* for the 1957 TR3 test car, but after 20 years there was no way of checking on the original data. The actual weight was more likely to be in the range of 2,160lb to 2,180lb.

One thing brought out is that any four-cylinder TR (pre-TR7, of course) is just about as quick as any other, though top-gear performance of the TR4 and TR4A models was significantly improved. As one has always thought, the earliest TR2s were the most economical of all.

Fastest and most powerful, it goes without saying, were the non-federal fuel-injected TR5s and early TR6s, which gave a genuine 120mph top speed.

(Tables on next page.)

	TR2	TR3 hardtop	TR4	TR4A	TR5	TR6	TR7 coupe	UNITED STATES 'FEDERAL' SPECIFICATION CARS			
								TR250	TR6	TR7	TR8** V8
	1,991cc with o/d	1,991cc with o/d	2,138cc	2,138cc with o/d	2,498cc	2,498cc with o/d	1,998cc 4-speed	2,498cc	2,498cc	1,998cc	3,528cc
Mean maximum speed (mph)	103	102	102	109*	120	119	109	—	—	—	120
Acceleration (sec)											
0-30mph	3.6	3.7	3.7	3.5	3.1	2.8	3.2	4.0	4.0	4.3	2.9
0-40mph	—	—	5.8	6.0	4.6	4.5	4.5	5.6	5.6	6.1	4.2
0-50mph	8.2	8.8	8.3	8.3	6.5	6.3	6.7	8.6	7.6	7.6	6.2
0-60mph	11.9	12.5	10.9	11.4	8.8	8.2	9.1	10.6	10.7	11.3	8.4
0-70mph	15.9	16.6	14.7	16.0	12.5	10.8	12.9	—	14.3	15.5	11.1
0-80mph	22.3	22.4	20.9	23.1	16.0	15.2	17.0	20.0	20.0	20.5	14.0
0-90mph	31.5	33.8	28.2	30.8	21.4	20.2	22.8	—	—	27.9	18.8
0-100mph	51.9	—	46.3	48.8	28.5	29.0	32.1	39.0	39.0	—	24.4
Standing ¼-mile (sec)	18.7	18.7	17.8	18.5	16.8	16.3	17.0	17.8	17.9	18.5	16.3
Direct top gear (sec)											
10-30mph	9.4	—	—	—	8.6	—	—				
20-40mph	9.3	9.6	8.2	9.0	7.4	6.9	8.0				
30-50mph	9.3	10.2	8.5	8.0	7.5	7.0	7.5				
40-60mph	9.5	11.0	8.8	8.1	7.6	7.3	7.2				
50-70mph	10.4	12.5	9.4	9.2	7.6	7.7	7.9				
60-80mph	11.4	14.5	10.3	10.8	8.5	8.5	9.0				
70-90mph	14.5	16.8	12.7	13.7	10.9	10.6	10.3				
80-100mph	—	—	25.4	31.4	15.2	14.5	15.2				
Overall fuel consumption (mpg)	32.0	24.9	22.5	25.4	19.6	19.8	26.4	27.5	25.9	34.4	18.5
Typical fuel consumption (mpg)	33	28	26	30	24	22	29	—	—	—	—
Kerb weight (lb)	2,100	2,464	2,184	2,358	2,319	2,473	2,128	2,350	2,360	2,355	2,655
Original test published	1954	1957	1962	1965	1968	1969	1976	1967	1969	1975	1980

*overdrive

**With 137bhp fuel-injection engine